Managing Your Cash Position

by Kenneth L. Parkinson

 Publishing

Hopewell, NJ

Published by:
Treasury Information Services
P.O. Box 99
Hopewell, NJ 08525

Orders:
Tel: 888-TIS-BOOK
Fax: 609-466-0091
www.tisbooks.com

Published 2008
Printed in the United States of America
ISBN 1-880423-02-2

Table of Contents

Acknowledgments

Disclaimer

Preface · 7

1. Cash Management: Home of the Cash Position · · · · · · · · 9

2. What Is a Cash Position? · · · · · · · · · · · · · · · · · · · 19

3. The Starting Place: Cash Central · · · · · · · · · · · · · · 27

4. What Goes into Your Cash Position? · · · · · · · · · · · · 41

5. Using a Cash Position Worksheet · · · · · · · · · · · · · · 53

6. Harnessing Cash Flows· 65

7. The Need for Accurate Cash Flow Forecasts · · · · · · · · · 87

8. Global Cash Positions · · · · · · · · · · · · · · · · · · · 105

9. Getting Started · 115

Appendix A: Short-term Investing · · · · · · · · · · · · · · · 123

Appendix B: Short-term Borrowing · · · · · · · · · · · · · · · 129

Appendix C: Reconciliation and Positive Pay Services · · · · 133

Appendix D: Guidelines for Using Technology · · · · · · · · 135

Glossary of Treasury Management Terms · · · · · · · · · · · 137

About the Author · 153

Acknowledgments

I would like to thank Ray Ruzek for suffering through an earlier version of this book. His feedback was very useful and has, I believe, helped to make this a better book.

I also want to thank my partner, Joyce Ochs, for her tireless editing, layout, design, and publishing prowess. She never fails to improve greatly anything I write. Her insights and reader's point of view are invaluable assets.

Disclaimer

The author and the publisher have used their best efforts in the preparation of this book and in providing accurate and up-to-date information. This book is sold with the understanding that the publisher and the author are not engaged in rendering legal, accounting, or other professional services. If any of these services are required, readers should seek the services of competent professionals.

Every effort has been made to make this book as complete a possible. However, there may be mistakes, both typographical and in content. It should also be noted that the information in this book is current only up to the printing date.

The author and the publisher shall have neither liability nor responsibility to any person or entity with respect to any loss or damage caused, or alleged to have caused, directly or indirectly, by the information in this book.

If you do not wish to be bound by the above, you may return this book to the publisher for a full refund.

Preface

In my teaching and training experience I have often noted that many cash managers, whether new to the field or more experienced, often fail to understand the importance of their companies' cash positions. Instead, they focus on the cash flows, sometimes ignoring the bigger picture. Many of the text books and other published material about cash management reflect this approach.

My intention in this book was to take a different tack in looking at cash management. I hope to help managers in organizations of all sizes come up to speed or get a fast refresher course in cash management. Even if you're a seasoned cash manager, I believe there is something for you in this book—e.g., a confirmation that your current system is as good as it can get or recognition that you can modify what you're doing to make your system more efficient.

I believe that cash management is done best when it is simple. Your goal should be to get rid of any cumbersome, inefficient practices. You need to get control over your cash flows to manage cash well. The approaches I discuss in this book should help you with your mission.

Kenneth L. Parkinson
Hopewell, NJ
July 2008

1

Cash Management: Home of the Cash Position

The cash management function is the pivotal point in a company for pooling cash collections, routing those funds to where they are needed, or parking excess funds where they will earn interest (or save interest expense) while they are not needed. A cash management system is designed to manage the cash flows of an organization—cash collections, disbursements, and concentration—and to selectively use short-term investing or borrowing to maintain target cash levels. A good cash management system also provides information to company financial managers to help them anticipate future liquidity needs.

To be effective, the cash manager requires ongoing information. Internally, it is necessary to know the firm's immediate and short-term cash needs and to be able to fill those needs without creating a panic situation. Externally, it is important to determine what funds have been received or need to be funded in the company's bank network. This requires an information system that combines information from many sources into a central report from which actions can be taken.

The Cash Management Function

Cash management systems have to be manageable, or they will not work well. Manageable usually means a limited number of banking relationships and bank accounts, efficient use of funds transfer services, and reasonable costs for necessary banking services. For this reason, cash managers should constantly be looking for newer, cost-effective services from their banks.

The daily challenge for the cash manager is managing the company's cash position—i.e., assuring that the company can balance its cash daily inflows and outflows. To do this requires timely and accurate information. In fact, some people maintain that cash management is, in actuality, the management of *information* about cash.

Managing the cash position essentially means keeping a "running score" on daily cash flows. The challenge lies in the collection of this information in time to act on it effectively. For example, receiving information about a deposit too late to transfer the funds renders the information valueless.

A company's overall cash management function is the environment that houses the company's cash position. How effectively a company's cash position is managed will be determined by how well its cash flows are managed. A solid cash management system ensures that valuable cash flow information is available on time and in the right format.

A cash manager's responsibilities

The duties of a cash manager can be different because of company size and organization, but in most cases, there are common responsibilities. A cash manager's duties typically include the following activities.

Monitoring the daily cash position

On a daily basis, the cash manager typically spends the first part of the day developing the cash position. The goal of this exercise is to identify shortages and surpluses in time to either borrow funds to cover the shortfall or invest excess funds. The cash manager first confirms the prior day's closing balance, typically using on-line or Internet bank reporting. Forecasted and scheduled disbursements, receipts, loan repayments, and maturing investment proceeds are then added and subtracted to calculate the day's cash flow. The cash manager also typically administers the credit facility, borrowing on a day-to-day basis. This daily reconciliation process also provides an effective method of immediately revealing unauthorized or fraudulent transactions.

Controlling balances on deposit

The cash manager maintains bank balances at a level adequate to avoid overdrafts and to compensate the bank for cash management services. Short-term borrowing may be necessary to meet the required balances. Excess funds are typically invested, short- or long-term, until they are required to cover capital or operating expenditures.

Moving funds as necessary

The cash manager may control several different bank accounts, perhaps in different states or even foreign countries. The transfer of monies from one account to another is often a daily exercise to prevent cash shortages in the accounts and to make sure surpluses are invested promptly .

Managing short-term borrowing and investing

Whether a company is an overall investor or borrower, the unsynchronized timing of operating cash flows (working capital) requires the cash manager to be both a borrower and an investor. On any given day, the cash manager may borrow to meet short-term cash requirements or invest surplus cash.

Forecasting future shortages and surpluses

To determine the amount and various maturities of the investment portfolio, the cash manager must predict future cash flows. Investing for a shorter period than necessary usually results in lost earnings, and investing for too long may cause premature security sales at a loss if funds are needed before maturity. Forecasting also allows the cash manager to plan for an adequate level of short-term credit facilities.

Managing banking relationships

The cash manager maintains a mutually beneficial relationship with the company's bankers. If the cash manager develops an open and straightforward relationship, the banker can develop a good understanding of the company's operations and can bring relevant banking products and services to the attention of the cash manager.

Performing analytic reviews and feasibility studies of banking services

The cash manager is the employee with primary responsibility for evaluating the benefits and drawbacks of adding new or terminating existing banking services. A company selects a bank that offers reliable, cost-effective services. The cash manager is responsible for monitoring the bank's services and fees to ensure that the arrangement remains satisfactory and that pricing is contractually accurate.

Analyzing, designing, and implementing cash management systems and procedures

Cash managers have a professional responsibility to keep up-to-date on developments in cash management products and practices by attending conferences, reading journals, and other networking and continuous learning activities. While growing professionally, the cash manager acquires and updates the skills and knowledge necessary to implement the cash management systems and procedures best suited to the company objectives.

Cash management structure

Key "anchors" of good cash management include blending transaction processing for trade and payroll payments as well as financial activities with managing the organization's overall liquidity prospectively. Good cash management also entails establishing an efficient banking network company-wide. Much cash management activity involves information management— obtaining data at the beginning and throughout the business day and working with company-wide cash flow forecasts.

The broad benefits of effective cash management include the effective use of internally generated cash, better short-term investments, optimized short-term borrowing, more effective banking relationships, and reliable cash flow forecasting.

Major influences on cash management structure

There are several factors that determine how a company can establish an efficient cash flow management system. In most cases, the central treasury function may not be able to dictate how the company collects from customers or pays its vendors. What it can do, however, is use the best services and techniques associated with the company's payment configuration. The critical factors that financial managers must consider are discussed below.

Organization

The way a company is organized with respect to its payment flows (in and out) heavily influences the types of services or techniques it can use. For example, a retail company can be defined as one that receives most if not all of its payments at the point of sale, such as a department store or fast food chain, or at the point of purchase, such as a mail-order firm or an Internet-based "e-tailer". Such companies would not use a bank lockbox service because this service only is justified when customers mail in their remittances. A retail company should be focused on how to expedite deposits quickly and economically, such as using the multiple branches of a large interstate bank whose footprint covers a wide geographic area.

Interest rates and the transitional time value of money

Interest rates affect how important it is to clear checks faster, consolidate funds into concentration pools, and disburse funds efficiently. If interest rates are 8%, clearing checks faster provides higher economic value than when interest rates are 4%. The time it takes to clear and consolidate funds is the *transitional time value*—i.e., the time it takes for funds in the company's collection "pipe line" to become usable at a point where the funds can be redeployed to pay the company's suppliers, employees, etc. The primary goal in constructing an efficient cash flow management system is to provide a simple system that consolidates funds and controls the outflow of funds with little manual intervention by the financial manager or other treasury staff.

Bank service charges

Bank service charges are no longer a minor expense item. This has changed the nature of many corporate-bank relationships. For instance, in many cases when a bank is considering a company's request for a new line of credit or to renew an existing line, the bank will expect additional cash management service business, or it may not offer the line at all.

Attitudes toward bank services

There is a steady trend toward using fewer banks. With many of today's banks offering multiple collection points, companies have found it possible to function effectively with one bank that has been chosen through a competitive bidding process.

Technology and the Internet

The Internet has become the chief medium for gathering data from company banks, for communicating with banks and other company locations, and for researching financial information and services. In addition to the Internet, the use of imaging technology by banks offers accelerated transfer of information from the bank to its customers.

In developing and maintaining an efficient system, the financial manager must be able to tap into the opportunities offered by these factors. The final result should be the "best" practices for each of the major areas—cash collections, cash concentration, cash disbursements, and managing bank relations.

Using bank services

Banks can help in building effective cash management systems. They offer services that provide:

- Information about cash flows within the bank's control (e.g., funds concentrated, checks deposited or paid, electronic transfers made or received).
- Ability to make electronic transfers to move company funds to points where funds are required.
- Concentration of funds from deposit banks (or accounts with the same bank) for use in funding disbursements or other uses of cash.
- Accelerated clearing of check deposits and reporting of this information to the company.
- Simplified and controlled funding of disbursement accounts.
- Protection against check fraud.

Bank services alone will not give a company an effective cash management system. To develop an effective cash management system, companies must have an internal system to process to process the bank information and to react to problems immediately. The combination of external bank-supplied services, with efficient internal operating procedures and reporting, forms the substance of a good cash management system for any company.

Developing an Efficient Framework

An effective cash flow management system should be a simple one with logical steps and easily identified flows. A typical system is shown below.

Exhibit 1.1 An Efficient Cash Management System

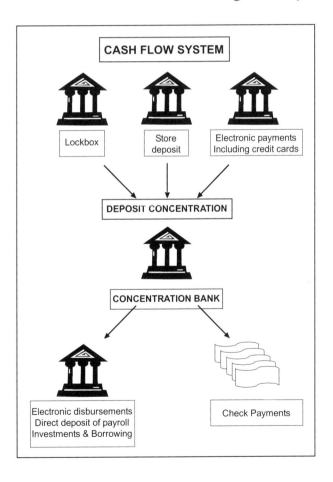

The simplified figure shows several things:

- There is a simple flow from deposit points to the concentration bank. No interruption is necessary. The deposits can be concentrated by ACH (debit) transfer.

- There is a clear consolidation into a central "pool" of cash from which funds can be redeployed to fund disbursements for vendors, payroll, taxes, investments, and loans, as applicable.

- The central pool clearly shows whether the company has excess cash to invest or needs to draw on one of the company's bank lines of credit.

- Cash disbursements can be handled centrally, with less chance of balances accumulating in local bank accounts.

Overall, the system is simple but can be expanded to include new points or arrangements with minimal disruption. It can also accommodate any form of payment.

Expanded information systems

Treasury managers have a continual need for information—both internally, from other operating or staff areas, and externally, from banks and third parties. Internal system integration was difficult to attain until post-2000, when many organizations jettisoned their old, limited systems for newer ones that promised connectivity throughout the organization. Today, integration is more common and feasible.

Size has dictated much of the development of new, multi-functional systems, such as enterprise resource planning (ERP) systems that larger organizations have been implementing over the past few years.

ERP systems have delivered the integration in many financial and operational areas, but in some cases—and treasury is the major exception—the integration required additional or substitute modules (often referred to as "bolt-ons") to enhance or replace the corresponding ERP module. Even if ERP systems have not completely delivered on their promise of company-wide integration, they represent a large step in that direction.

Larger companies have also implemented treasury management systems, usually in the form of a treasury work station to help handle their large amounts of data. In smaller firms, spreadsheet models are the most common method of handling treasury management information needs.

In addition, to ERP and treasury work station systems, redesigned financial systems have enabled financial managers to obtain better information and get clearer pictures of transactions. New payment formats, such as ARC and IRD (discussed in a later section below), and faster processing, such as in settlement time or in hours that systems are available, provide much more information about transactions and positions than was possible previously.

More and more applications are moving to the Web. This makes it essential that financial managers understand how the Web works and know how to tap into Web resources quickly and efficiently. This will be explored further in the next chapter.

Account analysis statements

One of the most important reports that banks provide to companies is a bank account analysis statement, which differs from a monthly bank account statement. An account analysis statement is usually provided monthly for every account a company maintains with the bank. It provides a recap of the prior month's activities, showing average balances maintained, values for those balances (earnings credits), and itemized service charges.

You should remember that your account analysis statements are excellent sources of information about your cash management system. They show volumes for all banking activities, all the services the bank provides, and the average balances you maintained at the bank for the past month.

These statements are "must" reading for cash managers and others involved with bank compensation. Statements have to be checked for accuracy to assure that the bank's data are correct. In addition, since the analysis statements show all the services the bank has provided for the past month, a cash manager can use these statements to see if the company is using services it does not need or if a requested account closing or service elimination was not completed.

As soon as possible, a cash manager should review with the company's banks any errors, discrepancies, or other questionable items to resolve them. Questions or problems that linger only become more time-consuming and difficult to resolve.

The In-house Bank

One other approach to treasury management that is gaining in popularity among large companies and some of the middle-market companies with global business is the *in-house bank*. This arrangement establishes the central treasury group as the financial center for the overall corporation.

With an in-house bank, the operating units, domestic and foreign subsidiaries, and other staff departments are required to deal with the central treasury group (the "bank") for all financial transactions. This grants a great deal of responsibility and power to the central group as it handles everything from funding accounts to making foreign trades and managing the global cash position(s).

2

What Is a Cash Position?

It's 10:00 AM. Do you know where your cash is? Do you know how much cash your organization has available to use? What cash flows—in and out—are you expecting today? Tomorrow? Next week?

If you are responsible for managing your organization's cash, you are responsible foremost for the organization's cash position. You must be able to answer these questions.

The primary function of your treasury group is to make sure the organization has enough cash every day to keep running smoothly. When you hear news stories that quote a corporate treasurer as saying that his or her firm has just a few days' cash left, it probably means that the company is going to seek bankruptcy protection.

Organizations of all types and sizes have to manage their cash positions daily. How well they do this determines how efficiently their organizations function from day to day. Focusing on the cash position keeps your focus on treasury's prime function—maintaining a stable liquidity level for the overall organization.

Does Size Count?

Company size often affects how complex managing your cash position is because larger companies tend to require more services and may have more banks to deal with. Because of their heavier volumes and multiple banking relationships, larger companies have bigger information systems needs. They are the primary market for treasury work stations, which provide automate support for treasury activities, including cash position management.

Smaller companies may have simpler systems, at least at first glance. The real problems for smaller firms are their ability to adjust to substantial changes in their cash flows and their limited resources, such as lines of credit or sizable investments. Smaller companies may also differ from their larger counterparts in that financial managers in small companies often are called upon to perform many tasks, whereas their counterparts in larger organizations are more specialized.

Real-time Finance

Working in treasury is challenging because you are dealing with finance in a real-time situation for much of the business day. The treasury group typically interacts with banks, the money markets, operating units throughout the company both domestically and abroad (if applicable), and other corporate staff departments, such as accounting, purchasing, inventory, and internal audit.

Obviously, the size of the organization will determine how intensely treasury staff must interact with the money markets and other internal personnel throughout the business day. Smaller companies may not immediately recognize the need to be that active throughout the day. They simply check their balances and other factors less frequently than treasury managers with larger companies. Managers in smaller companies do not understand the need to stay on top of the market.

The organization's cash position has to be managed every day that funds are available; i.e., every business day that the banks are open. This is the first order of business. Other tasks must be worked in around this key activity.

Cash flows can vary from day to day, and cash inflows do not often balance with cash outflows. The mix of cash flow items can change daily as well, depending on regular processing and payment cycles. The magnitudes of cash flow items can also vary widely over time, affected by seasonal factors or payment cycles. Regardless, the goal in managing the cash position is to make sure that the overall net position at the end of each day is positive.

Obviously, you cannot rely on the operating cash flows of your organization to balance daily. Financial sources of cash or places to "park" cash for a short-term period (even as often as overnight) are necessary. There also must be planning to arrange short-term borrowing facilities if funds are needed. Similarly, you will probably want to gain more familiarity with possible short-term investments when you have excess funds that are not needed on the current business day.

Collecting data

A company's cash position, in its simplest form, is obtained when cash outflows, including any debt repayments, are subtracted from cash inflows, including any maturing investments. Managing the cash position includes pulling all the data about operating and financial cash flows together throughout the business day, as well as from day to day.

This data gathering should be a fairly simple process as long as all sources of cash flow data are identified and tapped for information. These sources can be internal to the company, ranging from central financial departments to operating divisions and subsidiaries. Data sources can also be external points, such as the organization's financial services providers. If the latter are diverse, the system for collecting their data will be complex and possibly quite time consuming.

For small changes or simple additions, you will probably have to resort to a spreadsheet model or a group of them linked together in a workbook. If you can develop these models yourself, that can be an asset. If not, you will need help from your IT group or possibly outsource it to an external firm.

In cases large or small the key is for you to provide appropriate documentation to the systems technical experts. You cannot expect your IT group or an external outsourcing firm to know what's in your head. You will need to provide the specifications for your new system if you want to have it completed properly.

What are we talking about here?

The easiest way to see the impact of cash management is to look at the cash position. The flows in Exhibit 2.1 are shown in two parts—inflows and outflows. There are many possible cash flow components, but the general classifications shown here should cover them. I have also included a brief comment on each component related to the large-, mid-market- and small-sized organizations. Note that all these flows do not occur daily.

You can add more detail to these components to reflect your situation. However, it is critical that you identify all major cash flows that will affect the overall cash position for your organization. This is true even if the individual flows are not daily.

The cash position should be the central hub for the company's short-term financial flows. Determining the organization's cash position at its major bank (or banks) is the starting and ending place for daily cash management decision-making. This activity is most effectively managed on a centralized basis and takes priorities over other treasury tasks until it is completed. While it is not a glamorous part of a treasury manager's job, managing the cash position is a necessary element for a smooth-running financial function. Done well, this activity blends in well with other daily activities. Done poorly, it can create significant headaches for the treasury staff.

If this daily activity is not being ably managed, the overall organization is likely to suffer. This can especially be true in large, decentralized organizations where local financial managers are accustomed to handling payments and receipts. This can create an inefficient system, but even a company with an inefficient cash management system can still function if it manages its overall cash position effectively. However, if such a company cannot manage its cash position effectively, it will face substantial problems and threats to its ability to survive any financial crises.

Exhibit 2.1 Major Components of the Cash Position

CASH INFLOWS	Large Company	Mid-market Company	Small Company
Customer check payments from lockboxes	Large amounts	Mixture of large and small size	Smaller check size
Customer check payments from field deposits	Heavy volume if decentralized	Moderate volume	Not for small businesses
Customer check payments received at the head office	Light volume if decentralized	Moderate volume	Moderate to heavy volume
Customer check payments from point of sale (depends on industry)	Heavy volume	Moderately heavy volume	Smaller volume, if any at all
Customer check payments from remote capture and over-the-counter deposits	Heavy volume	Moderate volume	Not much
Wire transfers from customers	Can be heavy	Moderate volume	Not much
Wire transfers from subsidiaries	Moderate volume	Small volume	Not much
International wire transfers	Can be heavy	Small volume	Not much
Maturing short-term investments	Substantial amount possible	Moderate amount	Very small amount
Liquidation of assets	Large potential	Moderate potential	Small potential
Short-term borrowing proceeds	Large amounts possible	Moderate amounts possible	Small amounts possible
Long-term financing proceeds	Substantial	Infrequent	Rare
Proceeds from sale of assets (e.g., accounts receivable)	Large potential	Moderate potential	Small potential

CASH OUTFLOWS	Large Company	Mid-market Company	Small Company
Check payments to suppliers and other vendors	Large amounts	Mixture of large and small size	Smaller check size
Check and direct deposit (ACH) payments to employees	Heavy volume if not direct deposit	Moderate volume, possibly outsourced	Small volume, possibly outsourced
Payments to governmental entities (taxes)	Heavy volume	Moderately heavy volume	Smaller volume
Payments to others (retirees, shareholders, ST/LT lenders)	Heavy volume	Moderate volume	Not much
Wire transfers to customers	Can be heavy	Moderate volume	Not much
Wire transfers to subsidiaries	Moderate volume	Small volume	Not much
International wire transfers (outgoing)	Can be heavy	Small volume	Not much
Making short-term investments	Substantial amount possible	Moderate amount	Not much
LT investment transactions	Large potential	Small potential	None
Payback of ST debt	Large amounts possible	Moderate amounts possible	Proportion-ately larger
Payment of interest on debt	Substantial	Moderate	Proportion-ately larger
Repurchase of company securities (stocks, bonds)	Large amounts possible	Moderate potential	None

⇒ Get Started!

1. Using Exhibit 2.1 as a guide, create a spreadsheet "template" to record your daily cash flows.

2. Recreate a recent day's activities to see how easy or difficult it is to record data.

3. Review your recent history or try to identify all cash flows to be sure you have included them on your template.

4. Use the template daily in parallel with what you are doing today, determining if it needs to be adjusted.

5. If you are comfortable with your new template, begin using it.

6. Save each day's template in a master workbook by week.

3

The Starting Place: Cash Central

The easiest way to see the impact of cash management is to look at the cash position inputs to it daily. Exhibit 3.1 on the next page diagrams the relationships among the activities we normally associate with managing the cash position.

To understand more, you need to expand the blocks shown in the exhibit. For instance, the "Starting Bank Positions" block has at least two components—your expected position from the previous business day and the reported start-of-business-day balances for the current business day, which you receive via bank information reporting services (either directly or through your treasury work station). You will have as many starting positions as you have major banks that command attention daily. The overall starting position is the net sum of all the individual positions at each bank. It follows that it is much simpler to manage a system with few major banks, and this is what you should strive for.

Similarly, the "Planned Tasks and Forecasts" block incorporates other cash flows—real or just possible—as well as your rolling daily cash forecast into your daily routine. You cannot manage the cash position effectively if you do not have reliable

Exhibit 3.1 Cash Central

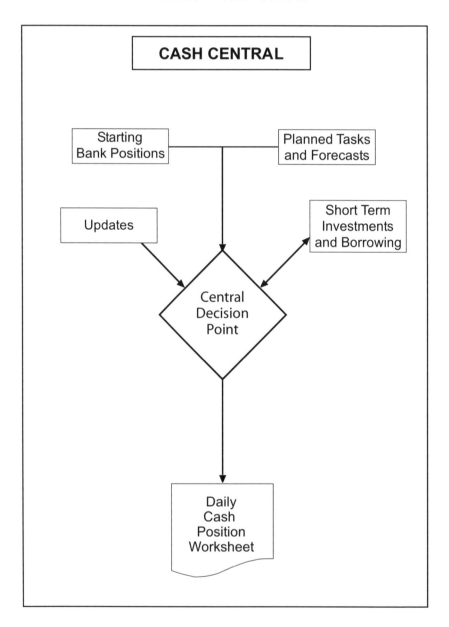

short-term projections of your cash needs and surpluses. This is critical regardless of the size of your organization.

The activities are brought together into the decision point, which changes dynamically throughout the business day as cash flows are identified and handled. During the business day there are updates to the cash forecast as well as "surprises," unplanned cash flows that usually demand some action in real time.

In essence, all this filters into the daily cash position. The cash position worksheet is an ongoing record of managing the position throughout the business day.

Exhibit 3.1 generally holds for organizations of any size, but there are a few differences due to size of the organization. For example, large corporations with intricate networks and multiple reporting sites would use a treasury work station for consolidating the information to the central decision point. Large corporations also tend to have deeper resources in short-term investments and borrowing capacities they can tap into when needed. Smaller companies and many middle market companies do not have such available reserves. In addition, larger firms tend to have greater technical resources available to them than middle market or smaller firms.

The cash position may be managed by more than one individual. The number of people involved depends on the company's size and the global spread of its business units (defined in this case as any location that has a cash flow). Larger companies may have heavy volumes of transactions, so they require more than one cash manager and more information technology. Similarly, companies with many dispersed business units may require multiple cash position points. I'll discuss the effectiveness of these types of arrangements later in this chapter.

Bank information services can only report on activities within the bank's control, such as deposits, electronic transfers, disbursement account clearing, and concentration of funds. Maturing investments and/or loans are usually maintained in a separate, internal system that provides this information. Updates on current cash needs and excesses come from separate communications with the source of these needs or excesses. Managing the cash position, then, is pulling all this information together throughout the business day, as well as from day to day.

The cash position is a critical point for companies of *all* sizes. You can think of it as the company's point of liquidity. There is just one overall point. If you can recognize more than one point, your liquidity management may be ineffective and may be costing your organization (more on this later).

Today's changing treasury systems environment has new needs and requirements. Organizations are moving from transaction initiation with a single bank back to a multibank environment, driven by standards (e.g., the BAI format, Microsoft Windows, the Web). There is also a strong need to link treasury systems into other corporate systems to satisfy some of the treasury information needs that all organizations have. Current systems need to keep up with and accommodate this desire for integration. Most of the current technology can be broken down into three areas—payments, treasury systems, and the Internet. I have included a short checklist in Appendix D that can help you get the right mind set for approaching technology.

The Internet (or more specifically, the Web) has provided common ground for service providers and users. For providers it has offered a cost-effective medium or platform to deliver information-based reporting and individually initiated transactions. For users it has provided a consistent format that allows for simple learning and start-up as well as housing sources for major technological developments that can be accessed by the knowledgeable "surfer."

Why Is This So Important?

Why start here? I believe that the daily cash position is the key financial activity for most organizations, so it makes sense to begin at this central point. It is true that you need an effective cash management system and a system for processing payments into and out of your organization. In the meantime, the company has to stay afloat. The cash position is your organization's major decision point regardless of how effective your cash management system is.

Without this major control point, you will tie up more cash than you need. In the past, most companies thought that large levels of cash on their balance sheets was a good sign of liquidity. It seemed to make sense: the more cash and cash equivalents (which are combined on the balance sheet) showing on the balance sheet, the more liquid the organization was, right? Most companies ultimately realized that just showing large amounts of cash on the balance sheet was no assurance that the company was in fact solvent because the cash might not be available to take care of the company's liabilities on a timely basis. They recognized, often with the help of their bankers or consultants, that their cash had to be mobilized and actively managed. This entailed establishing and managing a cash position daily.

It helps to have an overview, a big picture of the cash flows into and out of an organization as well as environmental factors that affect them. These are shown in Exhibit 3.2. In the exhibit, the

Exhibit 3.2 Overview of the Cash Position

CASH POSITION FACTORS

INFLOWS	RECEIPTS	CASH	PAYMENTS	OUTFLOWS
• Collections • Trade Credit • Discounted AR • Inventory Sales • Investment Income • Loan Draws				• Disbursements • Payroll Payments • Taxes • Loan Payments • Dividends • Investments
DRAGS • Uncollected Receivables • Obsolete Inventory • Low Investment Rates • Lax Credit Management				**PULLS** • Early Payments • Shortened Credit Limits • Limited Credit Lines • Low Liquidity Position

cash inflows section lists the major types of incoming funds flows. It also shows the drags on these flows; i.e., the factors that can reduce cash inflows by delaying cash receipts or diminishing the return on an investment. If the drags are significant, the expected cash inflows may be decreased, hurting the organization's overall cash position. Note that improving or eliminating the drags brings in more cash

Opposite the cash inflows section are the cash outflows. They are typically payables disbursements (shown as just "Disbursements"), payroll, etc. The outflows section lists factors that can "pull" payments through faster than normal. This can use up a valuable liquidity "cushion" before its planned use. Like the drags on inflows, the pulls on outflows can be important if they grow in magnitude. Improving the pulls, such as by paying in a more timely fashion or extending credit limits to good customers, improves short-term liquidity by extending your use of cash.

What Goes Into the Cash Position?

How involved a cash position is will depend on the elements discussed below. While size does have an obvious effect—i.e., larger organizations tend to have larger-sized payments and transaction volumes. However, the elements of the cash position are similar regardless of size. They include:

- The overall cash balance—across all banks, rolled up to the point where the funds can be mobilized. You cannot roll up beyond this point, or you will run into trouble.

- The expected flows—the shortest-term estimate. This is tighter and has to the most accurate forecast you can develop.

- Daily activity—changes to the position. (See sidebar below.)

- The buffers—what are these? They may include short-term investments (usually overnight), short-term sources of funds (i.e., bank lines of credit), other pools of funds.

- The surprises—you cannot avoid these, unfortunately.

Time Line For Managing the Cash Position	
8:00 AM to 9:00 AM	Bank balance information gathered and assimilated
11:00 AM	Updates and contacts finished
11:00 to 12:00 noon	Decisions made; funds transferred
3:00	Paperwork and confirmations done
4:00	Plan for next business day

A time line such as this should not be tough to establish. You may ruffle a few feathers of those who are used to calling their own shots but will no longer be able to do so. Change is not easy to bring about and finalize.

There are any number of aids and resources that assist in managing the cash position. These include simple spreadsheet models, bank information reports that show summary and detailed information for key accounts, and advanced treasury systems that gather, process, and present information for you to use in managing the cash position. Treasury work stations are recommended when you have a complex organization that requires a large number of bank accounts and a large number of regular funds transfers.

Simplify, Simplify!

Your underlying objective, regardless of your size, should be to streamline the cash flows of your organization. Organizations of all sizes fall into the trap of too much human intervention in managing the cash position. This cash "congestion" ties up cash in the system that would otherwise be available for use. As a result, there can be lost investments, excessive short-term borrowing, and unnecessary funds transfers. Cash management systems do not have to be overly complex; the simpler the system, the easier it is for funds to move smoothly and cheaply.

How do these systems become so complex? Over time cash management systems get complicated gradually as new business units are created or acquired. It is easy to just add a new service and add it to the existing system. Ideally, the occasions when a

Illustration: Streamlining a System

You have been asked to evaluate a mid-to-large-sized company's cash flow system. The system is old, and the new treasurer and CFO think it can be improved. They also believe that the company's liquidity management will be improved by freeing up cash currently tied up in the company's cash flow "pipeline." The system is shown below.

What can we conclude here? Let's consider this banking system in four tiers:

- Tier 1: The lockbox banks (A, B, C, and D)
- Tier 2: The intermediate concentration banks (K and L)
- Tier 3: The active concentration banks (P and Q)
- Tier 4: The final bank (X)

On the face of it, funds seem to flow regularly, but there are some problems. The first thing that should hit you is that there are too many banks involved.

Having four lockboxes is inefficient; the Tier 1 banks can be reduced to one bank. Multiple sites with the same bank may be a possibility, but converting customers to pay electronically is a better idea.

As to the banks in Tiers 2, 3, and 4, they seem to be falling all over themselves. There is no good operational cash management reason to use 5 banks to concentrate funds when a single bank will do. Depending on the volume, customer locations, and size of the banks being considered, a single bank could possibly provide all the services now provided by nine banks. This would greatly reduce bank costs and would simplify managing the cash position. It would also allow the company to repay loans more often, reducing interest expense that can result if it borrowed needlessly for longer periods of time.

Do overbanked situations like this really happen? The answer is a qualified "yes." By that I mean they can develop over time if someone is not watching the

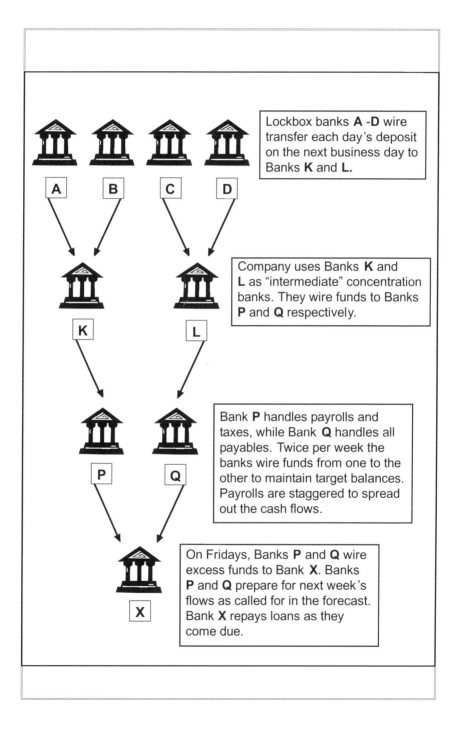

Lockbox banks **A** -**D** wire transfer each day's deposit on the next business day to Banks **K** and **L**.

Company uses Banks **K** and **L** as "intermediate" concentration banks. They wire funds to Banks **P** and **Q** respectively.

Bank **P** handles payrolls and taxes, while Bank **Q** handles all payables. Twice per week the banks wire funds from one to the other to maintain target balances. Payrolls are staggered to spread out the cash flows.

On Fridays, Banks **P** and **Q** wire excess funds to Bank **X**. Banks **P** and **Q** prepare for next week's flows as called for in the forecast. Bank **X** repays loans as they come due.

big picture. A new lockbox bank may seem feasible, but it must be considered as part of the overall system. Too often this is not done.

Sometimes systems like this one develop because of other factors that cannot be controlled. A good example is when a company is facing a critical financial situation and may be required to deal with a few select group of banks. In the past, this might have meant that the company might not be able to establish an up-to-date system with the latest bank services. However, wide variations in core cash management services have really decreased to the point where any customer can obtain up-to-date services.

new unit is brought into the overall system should be used to take a look at the overall system to determine whether it needs an overhaul.

You'd be surprised at how often people are willing to work with existing, complicated, time-consuming systems. This is especially true in smaller and middle-market firms. Because there are fewer people involved, the treasury manager has multiple responsibilities beyond managing the cash position. Somehow, the job gets done. After a while, managers adapt to their inefficient systems, but often they have little time for anything else.

To simplify, you must take a step back to look at the bigger picture. A good time to do this is when you are working, but it's a bank holiday. Since you do not have to scramble to manage your cash position, you have time to scrutinize your system. You probably know as well as any consultant what tasks are overly time-consuming. You may not be able to change how things are done right away, but by looking at a bigger picture, you should be able to identify what needs to be changed.

For example, does your system require a great deal of interaction between the banks, treasury staff, other corporate departments, and operating units? How did this situation come about? Are there steps that could be automated or eliminated entirely? Your scrutiny of the current system should always be focused on making your system simpler and eliminating time-consuming tasks.

Dangers of Too Little and Too Much Cash

It may be appealing to keep cash levels at bare minimums, especially if your company is a heavy short-term borrower. However, if you keep cash levels too trim, you may run up against limited liquidity periods. Typically, it is the treasury manager's job to stay attuned to the market to see if liquidity sources are drying up and to take steps to store liquidity if necessary, before and after credit constraints occur.

If you are faced with too little cash, you usually have some type of short-term borrowing facility available or a short-term investment portfolio. However, if you also have an inefficient cash flow management system, you may have enough cash in the organization's pipeline that would eliminate the need to borrow the full amount of the cash imbalance. Pipeline cash may not cover all your short-term needs, but every unit of currency you save reduces the organization's interest expense and helps prevent illiquidity.

You might think too much cash cannot be bad. However, too much cash tends to encourage indifference among financial executives and can de-emphasize attention on the cash management activities, It can also create excess balances in bank accounts that are not given much importance by the company's financial managers.

Cash congestion

Large amounts of excess cash can create cash "congestion." Cash congestion occurs when there is far too much cash to be managed effectively. Some industries face this problem continually. For instance, the real estate-housing industry typically has multitudes of accounts because each property or group of properties has its own bank accounts to handle receipts, disbursements, and, often, investments. This can translate into dozens or even hundreds of bank accounts, which create this congestion because essentially the cash position for each property or group of properties must be managed separately. The more cash congestion there is in your system, the greater your potential loss.

Putting Together a Strategy

It seems as if everything you do in treasury is expected to have a strategy. I have never been a proponent of covering each activity with strategy, although I do think you need a strategy for how the cash position is managed. For example, your strategy could address the following questions:

How do you determine how many credit lines you will need over the next 12-18 months?

If you are a middle-market company or a large corporation, you may rely on credit lines to cover any negative cash positions. If this is the case, the lines need to be in place before they are needed. To determine the amount needed and probable timing, you have to develop a good projection of your cash needs. If you do not have a good forecast, you will probably have to err on the cautious side. This will cost your company the fees if the excess lines are not used. To determine how much in credit lines you may need, look back at your historical borrowing levels. A spreadsheet or graph is a good way of doing this. Remember that you will need to fund your highest daily cash need unless you can alter the cash flows to reduce any peaks in cash needs. If you are a smaller firm, you will probably not have any options with this.

How do you prepare the short-term cash forecast?

Forecasting must be an ongoing activity, especially as it relates to the very short-term forecasts that are vital in managing the cash position. Smaller companies may not believe that they need to spend much time with short-term forecasting. But it is necessary no matter what size your organization is. Daily forecasts have to be very accurate, or you will be unable to manage your cash position effectively.

How do you manage the balances at each of you major banks?

Here is where simplifying can pay big dividends in terms of treasury resources and manpower. This is more of a problem in larger companies having numerous baking relationships that must be actively managed. Even if you have a substantial number of accounts with the same bank, you can create an efficient framework by using zero balance accounts judiciously. This means that you can reduce the number of accounts that you have to manage to a small, manageable number.

How will short-term investments and/or short-term borrowing be handled?

For smaller and middle market companies, this is not a major headache, but it can be for larger firms. These two activities must work seamlessly with the manager of the cash position. You have to identify excess fund possibilities and roll them into short-term investments early in the business day to get the widest choice of instruments and interest rates. There also may be lead time involved in borrowing, so knowing your position as early as possible, even if it is a rough estimate, can mean a better borrowing rate because you may have time to shop around for the most attractive rate.

Who has the responsibility to change the company's cash management?

This is a key question, especially for larger firms, because the overall cash management arrangements dictate how difficult it will be to manage the cash position. The best arrangement is to have central responsibility for cash management as part of the corporate treasury group. This offers the most efficient structure. This structure may be easy to set up in smaller or middle market firms.

What about cash positions at foreign subsidiaries?

Managing these positions may be difficult for even the largest companies. It can be simpler at smaller corporations. However, you should still have a global strategy that can be administered on a local or regional level overseas if you have foreign customers and/or operations. Think of the foreign subs as smaller situations of the parent.

The end of this exercise should result in a plan for managing your cash position. Implementing the plan may take time and require additional assets, such as new systems, staff, or bank services. Having a plan can provide some stability in managing the cash position, an activity that can be frenetic at times.

In the past, it was not as easy to establish a simplified banking and cash management system. However, changes in the banking laws permitting interstate banking, the wider availability of bank products and services, technological innovations, and the Web have combined to simplify cash management and to make it easier to manage an organization's cash position.

What can middle market and small companies really do?

Smaller companies can also develop a cash position and streamline cash flows. For example:

1. Focus on streamlining your cash flows by tracking each major cash flow and eliminating any overlapping or inefficient practices and procedures.

2. Follow the cash! Remember your best source of cash is … your own cash. Don't leave it idling in your bank pipeline when you could be using it to add liquidity to your short-term activities.

3. If you have not been able to establish lines of credit, try improving your balance sheet and other financial statements before applying for new lines. For instance, go after obsolete inventory; hold the proceeds as cash or using them to pay down existing debt (always a good sign to your bankers).

4. Devote time to forecasting daily, weekly, and monthly cash flows. Do it often and measure its results regularly.

5. If you are chronically short of cash, consider discounting your current assets (inventory and receiv-

4

What Goes into Your Cash Position?

In this chapter we will delve deeper into the cash position to understand it better and to learn how to manage it more effectively. The topics in this chapter are fairly widespread and not all may apply to your case. However, at some point in time, I believe most of them will affect your managing the cash position.

The main "ingredients" for the cash position are balances (starting, ending, and perhaps in-between) and other related data (check clearings, deposits made but not yet cleared), financial activities (e.g., short-term investing and borrowing), forecasts, which contain a rolling maturity schedule, information on balances or other key data, and the number of banks used.

Cash Management and the Internet

Banks and cash management systems providers are currently in the process of adapting their software to the Internet. This has an impact on cash management operations both internally and externally.

Internally, many companies use Intranets to replace LANs and Wide Area Networks (WANs). Software applications and data are housed on a server and are accessed with a browser program. Whether cash management data are kept separate or not, cash managers use the Intranet to communicate with other company locations to share financial information.

Externally, the move to the Internet to communicate with other companies and with banks is where the greatest changes are occurring. Many banks have already or are in the process of moving access to information services to the Internet. This means that instead of having a computer retrieve data from the bank's information reporting system via a dial-up modem and specialized software, cash managers can use the Internet. Their account information will be accessible only to them at the bank's Web site.

Much of the day-to-day reporting that occurs today by telephone, computer, and fax machine will migrate to the Internet. Assuming sufficient space, it is easier for the bank to put all account-related data on the Web and let the customer access what is needed. This will work for imaged as well as traditional information reporting.

In addition to gathering data about their accounts, cash managers can also access many bank services via the Web. For instance, wire transfers and ACH transfers, which have been initiated using PCs with a telephone link to the bank, can now be initiated by companies at the bank's Web site. Cash managers are able to use a standard Internet browser rather than having to install specialized software for each bank service they use. Some banks are even adding international cash management services to their Web sites, enabling customers to initiate letters of credit or make cross-border transfers. This also helps the bank because it does not have to distribute new software to all its customers when the bank system is modified; it simply changes the software on the Web site.

In addition to bank access, the Internet may be changing some other traditional cash management transactions. Investments offered for auction, for example, are using the Web. Leasing companies are also beginning to move transactions to the Web.

The Internet is also a huge source of information for cash managers. Almost every bank has a Web site that contains information about its products and often also contains updates on key issues facing cash management. In addition to bank sites, a host of other sites from associations, consulting firms, universities, governments, and private individuals and companies provides information on countless topics and issues.

Currently, the volume of cash management transacted on the Internet is relatively small but will continue to grow. The Internet is changing how individuals and companies work, and it is likely to do the same for cash management. Expanded use of the Internet for bank-company communications and information transfer will improve not only cash management services but internal company systems, as well.

Balances

The main sources for cash position information are your banks. If you are fortunate to have only one bank or one major bank, it will be your lifeline when it comes to managing you cash position. In multi-bank situations, you will need to bring various pieces of data together (on the cash worksheet mentioned above) to obtain a consolidated cash position. Having global operations adds another dimension.

The types of data you will need include data from the previous business day and on occasion data from older days. Most of this information applies to your organization regardless of its size:

- Available balances for each account
- Funds movement details for each account
- Check clearings/postings for each account (especially those that are not controlled disbursement accounts, which are discussed below)
- Returned items (checks or ACH transactions that were returned against your account)
- Other items, such as stop payment transactions or check inquiries

Other data items may be more relevant for large corporations and larger middle market firms:

- Short-term borrowing transactions and balances
- Short-term investment transactions and balances
- International fund movements, including foreign exchange (FX) transactions and cross-border funds transfers,
- Custody balances for securities that the bank is holding on the company's behalf

Large companies and bigger middle market companies will also need to obtain same-day data from their bank or banks throughout the business day:

- Controlled disbursement clearings, which must be funded on the same business day
- Lockbox deposits, showing what has been deposited and when funds will be made available (today and over the next few says)
- Concentration reports showing what funds have been deposited today, which can be used to estimate cash inflows on the next business day
- ACH transactions (incoming and outgoing)
- Wire transfers, especially ones from foreign locations, such as Europe, which come in during the business day
- Positive pay reports and resolution of flagged items (checks) that failed to match against the positive pay file supplied to the bank

You may be able to get started with a summary report, such as the one shown in Exhibit 4.1

The previous-day portion is the part that you start with at the beginning of the day to reconcile yesterday's activities. The current day portion is the part you use to then continue with to-day's work. If you have no significant activity for the rest of the day, as is the case for small companies and smaller middle market firms, this report may be enough for you to manage your cash position. If you have further daily activity, you tap into a report like this as well as a detailed transaction report, which itemizes most large-dollar transactions.

Exhibit 4.1 Bank Information Summary Report

XYZ Bank

Bank Information Report

Summary Report

Country: USA   **Currency** USD ($)

Account Number Summary

Account name Summary

Previous Day	Ledger Balance	Available Balance	One Day Total	Two+ Day Total
Beginning Balance	5,467,589.28	4,100,691.96	1,093,517.86	273,379.46
Total Debits	1,450,675.55	1,450,675.55		
Total Credits	392,500.00	100,456.77	235,500.00	56,543.23
Closing Balance	4,409,413.73	3,042,516.41	1,329,017.86	329,922.69
Current Day	**Ledger Balance**	**Available Balance**	**One Day Total**	**Two+ Day Total**
Beginning Balance	4,409,413.73	3,042,516.41	273,379.46	0.00
Total Debits	2,455,263.82	2,455,263.82		
Total Credits	3,465,781.22	1,039,734.37	2,079,468.73	346,578.12
Closing Balance	5,419,931.13	4,053,033.81	2,352,848.20	346,578.12

There are many types of data that must be gathered and assimilated daily to manage the cash position effectively. Just one glitch can throw the position out of whack. It should be obvious that you want to keep your cash management system simple and not let your banking network become cumbersome.

In some cases using a treasury work station or some specialized software can make the data gathering and consolidation easier. However, too many bank accounts and activities can cause problems even for a work station.

Target balances

You may have instances when you want to or are required to leave balances with your bank. This could be to compensate the bank for cash management services provided or to keep mandatory compensating balances that must be maintained as part of a lending agreement.

Target balances are average levels of available (or collected) balances that are to be maintained with a bank. The targets are usually set by bank, not bank account, even though you usually will manage the target through a single master account. Imagine how difficult it is to manage target balances *by account*!

In managing your cash position, you treat balances as required cash, so it should appear as an outflow. Note that target balances remain as collected or available balances and are not included in any sweep account arrangements.

Residual balances

You should not expect to hit a zero ending balance for your cash position every day. In some cases you will have left-over (or *residual*) balances at the end of the day. If you do nothing, they will stay there and be available on the next day. If your company is a for-profit corporation, you will only be able to receive an earnings credit, which is not interest and can only be used to reduce your bank fees (think of it as a kind of gift card). To earn interest you must invest the funds by moving them to a dealer (this could be with the same bank) or set up a bank sweep arrangement.

Residual balances need to be included in your daily cash position management similar to target balances. Residual balances represent balances you cannot reduce easily; target balances represent funds that you are purposely leaving in your bank account. You should treat them as cash outflows, and you can include them as a fixed item in your daily cash forecast out as far as you like. At regular points, such as quarterly, you should analyze your residual balances to see if they can be reduced. It is always more efficient to try to eliminate residual balances and pay for bank services by fees if you can. This is because your short-term cost of funds is going to be greater than the bank's earnings credit rate or its sweep account rate, and you'll save the 10% reserve requirement that earns no earnings credit.

There are some exceptions, such as when rates drop very suddenly (sweep rates sometimes lag, making them temporarily very attractive) or if the amount you wish to roll into the sweep is substantial (e.g., over $10 million daily) and the bank agrees to increase its normal sweep rate to a money market rate.

Financial Activities

Major financial activities that can affect the cash position are short-term investing and borrowing. Short-term investing and short-term borrowing are key activities that can make managing the cash position easier if your company is large enough. These activities can seem fairly simple on the surface, but there is a lot more to them when you have to manage them on a daily basis. You also should be comfortable with both investing and borrowing because your organization may swing from a net invested position to a net borrowed position relatively quickly, and you need to be prepared.

Do not take imprudent risks with company assets. This "charter" is easy to understand with investments. Most companies are safe, conservative investors. There is usually an investment policy/guideline to give the financial manager who handles the investments a framework for the company's investments. It is prudent to conform to that policy daily.

Financial activities will have future implications unless you restrict all your activities to overnight maturities. (This is not a wise policy.) You also want to know how these activities affect the overall picture in terms of using up your debt capacity or monitoring the quality of your investments.

Financial activities may not be solely treasury's domain as other corporate groups or operating units can be given the ability to make investments or borrow. This is especially true for decentralized corporations, and it is often the case for multinational corporations with units in many foreign countries. In such instances it is impossible for the central treasury group to manage the overall position completely, and it must delegate the daily cash position management to local or regional staff. However, the cash positions of foreign subsidiaries can be monitored by the central treasury group, which can identify potential problems and suggest solutions. And, of course, you must have complete daily and intra-day information.

You should try to plan ahead for most of your financial activities because giving your lender or broker-dealer as much lead time as possible can get you a better rate. However, all financial activities cannot be planned. You really want to be prepared to handle the unplanned financial activities—the last-minute investment deal or drawdown on your line of credit—as easily as the planned ones. Obviously, you do not have the same expectations of desirable rates or maturities with unplanned activities.

Short-term investments

Companies that generate more cash than they need at the moment look for short-term investments where they can "park" those funds temporarily. Most cash managers are not trained investment money managers, and, as the amount invested can vary substantially over time, they look for very liquid (i.e., easily convertible into cash) investments with low risk.

Larger companies have more alternatives because they tend to have large enough amounts to invest in the money markets, thus enhancing their yields while still keeping risk down. They can do this with their banks, or they can deal directly with broker-dealer firms. Note that in the latter case funds must be transferred to the broker-dealer, while in the former, the funds are transferred within the overall bank. The costs of wires in and out may be insignificant for large-scale investments (multi-millions); it can be significant for smaller amounts or when interest rates are abnormally low (e.g., at 2% or lower).

Smaller companies and many middle market companies often take advantage of bank sweep investment arrangements. With this service, the bank is in essence giving you interest on your checking account balances by moving ("sweeping") them nightly into an investment account, where they earn interest, and transferring them back by the start of business on the next business day. These are popular services, but the main drawback is that the interest rate is usually quite low. Still, it does provide some value for otherwise-idle funds.

[For more details on short-term investment activities, see Appendix A.]

Short-term borrowing

Companies anticipating periodic cash shortfalls arrange for funds from their banks or from issuing money market securities. The most common form of short-term borrowing is an unsecured bank line of credit. Smaller firms may have to pledge assets to obtain a line of credit. Larger corporations tap the money markets for their short-term borrowings, but most of this is supported by backup lines of credit with their banks. In both cases, bank lines of credit provide the financial assurance that companies will have the funds when they need them.

Borrowing is a simple transaction, easily done with a phone call. To borrow under a line of credit, the company notifies the bank of its decision to do so and provides the bank with a note. The provision of notes for each borrowing can be eliminated by presigning a note for the full amount of the line (without drawing down any funds). Then, as funds are needed, they can be drawn against the presigned note. After the bank is notified, it transfers the funds into the company's bank account. Repayment is made by the company transferring the funds (plus interest) back to the bank on or before maturity. Loans can be rolled over in most cases. The transactions should show up in your daily bank report.

Smaller companies may face additional constraints imposed by their bank. For example, they may have to keep a percentage of the loan or even the overall credit line on deposit with the bank at all times. This is similar to a target balance discussed earlier. Small companies may also face a "cleanup" period, which is a period of time specified by the lender during which the company can have no outstanding loans. These provisions are negotiable to some degree. You have a better chance of eliminating them after you have shown that these provisions are not necessary in your case, and you do this by repaying your borrowings on time and by strengthening your balance sheet.

[For more details on short-term borrowing activities, see Appendix B.]

Influences on investing and borrowing

Outside influences may affect how well you are able to handle short-term borrowing and investing. Market changes, such as credit crunches or rapid changes in interest rates, can create problems for you if they occur without much warning. You need to re-view your alternatives regularly, so you are not caught short in times of financial stress.

Banking policies or shifts in economic policy by central banks can also be problem areas for you in managing the cash po-sition. In many of these cases, there is some warning, which al-lows you to make alternate arrangements. In such instances you may not be able to negotiate the best terms, but with enough lead time you should be able to set up facilities to be able to manage the cash position even if it may cost you a short-term loss in in-vestment rates or higher costs of short-term borrowing.

Strategies and policies

Whether you are a borrower or investor, you need a policy that provides appropriate guidelines. Examples of financial strategies are included in Appendix A and Appendix B. Standard strategies, such as passive or active ones, are satisfactory in most cases. Where they are not, they can still be used as starting points for new strategies. Once you have an acceptable strategy, it becomes a tool against which your performance will probably be mea-sured. You should be able to demonstrate—on demand—how well you are adhering to the strategy. For the most part, short-term investing and borrowing policies apply to larger com-panies and middle market companies. Smaller companies typi-cally do not have sizable enough investments or debt to require an elaborate policy.

Policies should offer working guidelines and reasonable protections for the company. They are intended to reduce the risks associated with financial activities. This may be more appli-cable for investment activities, where protecting the company's investment principal is a primary concern. In most cases cash managers tend to be careful about how much risk they will accept in an investment security.

⇒ Get Started!

You can create a cash position worksheet using the items shown in the following table:

Sample Cash Position Worksheet	
Available balances	
Lockbox deposits	
Over-the-counter deposits (today)	
Controlled disbursement clearings	
ACH transactions—credit transfsers	
ACH transactions—debit transfsers	
Funds movement—wire transfers made	
Funds movement—wire transfers received	
Check clearings/postings	
Returned items	
Positive pay checks returned	
Stop payments	
Short-term borrowing transactions	
Short-term borrowing balances	
Short-term investment transactions	
Short-term investment balances	
International funds movements— outgoing transfers	
International funds movements— incoming transfers	
FX funds transfers	

Note that you should eliminate the items that do not apply to your organization. Also you may have multiple entries daily for some of the items, such as wire transfers and controlled disbursement clearings. You can allow for this by leaving space on your worksheet or using a supplemental worksheet that posts the totals to your overall worksheet.

5

Using a Cash Position Worksheet

The cash position worksheet is a staple of cash position management. It may be on paper or in a computer spreadsheet. The worksheet should provide a working list of cash flow items that the cash manager uses to determine what cash management actions are required. The worksheet reflects the hub, or focal point, represented by the cash management function. As the blanks are filled in throughout the business day (usually early in the day), the company's cash position emerges.

It pays to be well organized if you want to manage the cash position effectively. Getting started you will need:

- *Previous day's worksheet*: This shows the expected balances (for today) at the close of business for the previous day and is used to reconcile the reported bank balances and transaction summaries from your banks (see below).

- *Short-term forecast*: You will need a rolling daily forecast for the next week at a minimum. The length of the forecast can be determined by the lead time it takes for you to complete a financial transaction, such as a short-term investment or borrowing, if one is necessary.

- *Updates*: These should come in during the early part of the day. Of course, you cannot really control their timing completely. Such surprises will test how resilient you are.
- *Bank balances*: You need these at the start of business and during the day.
- *Other "exceptional" cash flow items*: These may include the surprises (mentioned above) as well as transactions that are out of the ordinary, such as capital expenditures, long-term debt proceeds, etc.
- *Any bank target balances*: If you have set an average balance to be maintained at your bank(s), you will need to incorporate this target into your calculations when figuring the net position. In other words, you treat it as a cash outflow.

Daily reconciliation is a key activity because it helps identify any problems quickly. Done first thing every morning, it should allow you ample time to research and resolve any discrepancies, such as a transfer that did not occur or one that was erroneously credited to your account. Once all items have been reconciled, information can be sent to accounting for further handling.

The Cash Management Information Cycle (During the Business Day)

There is a normal cycle of cash management information that occurs daily.

In the early morning

Information from bank reporting systems is gathered and analyzed. This information shows the bank positions at the start of the business day. The prior day's activities are reconciled with the morning reports, and any discrepancies are researched and resolved right away. This morning reconcilement procedure initiates the business day for the cash management activity.

The starting worksheet should look like Exhibit 5.1. It shows the estimates and only the actual beginning balance ($22,150).

Exhibit 5.1 Daily Cash Position Worksheet (starting)

Time Period/Week of: xx/xx/xx	{Date}		
($ millions)	Current Day		
	Estimate	Actual	Variance (act-est)
Receipts/Inflows			
Beginning Balance	25,125	22,150	(2,975)
Staff deposits (remote capture)	1,500		(1,500)
Chicago lockbox	3,000		(3,000)
Atlanta lockbox	3,000		(3,000)
Maturing investments	10,000		(10,000)
Customer ACH payments	6,000		(6,000)
Miscellaneous cash inflows	1,000		(1,000)
International wires	8,000		(8,000)
TOTAL RECEIPTS/INFLOWS	57,625	22,150	(35,475)
Disbursements/Outflows			Variance (est-act)
Target Cash Balances	2,000		2,000
Controlled disbursements	7,500		7,500
Payroll: checks	8,650		8,650
Payroll: direct deposit	12,000		12,000
ST debt maturing	1,520		1,520
LT debt repayment	0		0
Miscellaneous cash outflows	2,500		2,500
Wires	8,750		8,750
TOTAL DISBURSMTS/OUTFLOWS	42,920	0	42,920
NET CASH FLOW/Ending Balance	**14,705**	**22,150**	**(78,395)**

The bottom-line variance (minus $78+ million is not meaningful until other data have been entered. The beginning balance is treated as an input. The net cash flow figure (last line) then becomes the ending balance for today and the beginning balance for tomorrow. Also, note how the variances are calculated so that a negative sign always means that the actual cash flow is less than expected. This will be more evident in the next exhibit.

As the morning continues

The cash manager receives information from company sources. These items usually involve a request for funds from locations that handle their own payments or are confirming a transaction, such as the amount of funds that were transferred to the parent's account on that business day. These funds are then available for use by the (central) cash manager.

Also during the morning

The cash manager receives updates from the company's bank(s) on current-day transactions. This includes the daily notifications for controlled disbursement clearings and positive pay exception items. The second notification (the total clearing amount) is the most important and is usually available before 11:00 A.M. (Eastern time). For positive pay, the deadline will depend on how much time the bank allows the company to respond.

Throughout the morning

The cash management staff is arranging short-term investments and/or loans, as necessary, through broker-dealers from their banks or investment banks. Much of this activity occurs before the final cash position of the day is reached. If a company is a substantial investor and uses one of its main banks for custody and safekeeping, its bank may be able to provide a daily report of the company's portfolio. If the company is a heavy borrower, it may be able to receive regular reports on daily borrowing activities from its banks. A company that is a substantial investor may subscribe to a service like Bloomberg or Reuters to receive real-time money market and other financial information.

Throughout the morning and up to the time that the wire transfer services close

The cash management staff makes funds transfers. This may be wiring out same-day funds from the lockbox account or unexpected wire transfers into the company's concentration account during the business day. For instance, transfers from foreign customers are likely to come in during the day, so cash managers who expect to receive funds in this manner check the bank accounts periodically. Finally, cash managers check for daily local deposit activity in retail collection situations. These reports show which locations did not report, so emergency actions can be taken. They also show the dollar amounts that will be available in the firm's concentration account on the next business day. This amount then becomes one of the numbers to verify the next morning.

Optimally, by mid-day

The cash movements for the day are completed or are scheduled for completion, and the company's cash position is finalized.

The cash position worksheet at this point should look like Exhibit 5.2 on the next page.. This has *all* the actuals filled in, indicating that the cash position for the day has been established. Note that these "actual" flows represent actions taken during the current day. They won't be officially "actual" until they are reconciled with tomorrow's report. Finally, note that the actual ending balance for today (+5,003) has become the beginning balance for the next day.

In the afternoon

All the necessary confirmation for all transactions is completed. Also, the running cash worksheet is updated and set for the next business day. This worksheet is where all activities are recorded and reconciled daily and may be manual or part of a cash management system.

This hypothetical schedule shows how important it is to have an efficient, smooth-flowing information system that can meet the time requirements. Departing from such a schedule usually results in a reactive, chaotic environment in which major problems occur with alarming frequency. For this reason, companies are always interested in ways that will help them streamline their information gathering and decision-making.

Exhibit 5.2 Cash Position Worksheet (Late AM/Early PM)

Time Period/Week of: xx/xx/xx		{Date}		{Date}
($ millions)	Current Day			Next Day
	Estimate	Actual	Variance (act-est)	Estimate
Receipts/Inflows				
Beginning Balance	25,125	22,150	(2,975)	5,003
Staff deposits (remote cap)	1,500	1,052	(448)	1,250
Chicago lockbox	3,000	2,748	(252)	2,000
Atlanta lockbox	3,000	3,497	497	5.000
Maturing investments	10,000	10,555	555	15,000
Customer ACH payments	6,000	4,831	(1,169)	7,000
Misc. cash inflows	1,000	975	(25)	2,000
International wires	8,000	5,625	(2,375)	10,000
TOT. RECEIPTS/INFLOWS	57,625	51,433	(6,192)	47,253
Disbursements/Outflows			Variance (est-act)	
Target Cash Balances	2,000	2,250	(250)	4,500
Controlled disbursements	7,500	8,545	(1,045)	6,000
Payroll: checks	8,650	8,575	75	2,500
Payroll: direct deposit	12,000	11,785	215	0
ST debt maturing	1,520	1,875	(355)	5,000
LT debt repayment	0	0	0	6,000
Misc. cash outflows	2,500	3,400	(900)	3,500
Wires	8,750	10,000	(1,250)	6,500
TOT DISBMTS/OUTFLOWS	42,920	46,430	(3,510)	34,000
NET CASH FLOW/ Ending Balance	**14,705**	**5,003**	**(9,702)**	**13,253**

Types of Cash Flows

Cash flows come in different forms, the amounts and types of each varying for individual organizations. Remember Exhibit 2.1, which showed the types of flows. A more defined set of cash flows should be adapted to your specific circumstances. For instance, your company may have many operating locations that handle their disbursements and upstream collections via lockboxes. They may have numerous operational cash flows daily, especially if more than one or two banks are involved. Similarly, if your company has highly centralized receivables and payables and frequent short-term borrowing (e.g., daily), you may have less operational transactions and more short-term financial transactions. Companies can also have long-term financial cash flows when they issue long-term debt or equity.

As these examples show, it is useful to categorize the types of cash flows:

- **Operational cash flows:** cash collections and concentration, cash disbursements, funds transfers among the organization's accounts, payroll funding
- **Short-term financial cash flows:** maturing and new investments, maturing and new short-term loans, payments associated with risk management instruments/hedges, interest income received and interest payments to lenders (short-term), foreign exchange purchases and sales
- **Long-term financial cash flows:** proceeds from long-term debt (e.g., bonds) and new equity issues (e.g., common stock or preferred stock), long-term investments, interest paid on long-term debt, dividends paid to shareholders and received from long-term investments, bond and/or stock repurchases

Using Spreadsheet Models

You may develop several types of spreadsheet models to help you manage the cash position. One useful type is the daily cash worksheet shown in Exhibits 5.1 and 5.2. You record each data item as it becomes available, constantly watching the bottom line—the cash position. You can use it to identify transactions that have not occurred as planned. You can also spot a large excess or deficit and take actions to invest or borrow as necessary.

Today's worksheet becomes the starting point for tomorrow's worksheet, and so on. This gives you an efficient reconciling tool. If your worksheet is in the form of a spreadsheet model, you can easily roll over from one day to the next. If your daily cash worksheet is overly complex, enhanced technology, such as a treasury work station, will probably be required.

Measuring variances is an important part of the daily routine. In the exhibit, I have calculated the variance as the actual amount minus the estimated amount for inflows and the opposite (estimates minus actuals) for outflows. I did this to use the negative signs (parentheses) to show differences that were detrimental—i.e., providing less cash than planned.

Synchronization

A goal sought by many treasury managers in organizations of all sizes is to match inflows with outflows daily. It's not always possible. Achieving this synchronization depends on how complex your information system is, how cumbersome your cash flows are, how seasonality affects your cash flows (in or out), and how efficient your cash management system is.

You should work with your banks and internal systems people to establish an effective information system regardless of your company's size. Getting better information may help you reduce the impact of awkward cash flows, although you should probably work to reduce their inefficiencies. Better information can also help you gauge the impact of seasonality and work out ways to minimize this impact. Better information can also help identify where your cash management system is not effective.

Float

One obstacle to improving your information flow is float. Whether collection float, disbursement float, or both, float is really an "enemy" of the treasury manager. You might not agree with this statement because you think disbursement float (i.e., *your* company's disbursement float) is a good thing. Well, I would argue that it is not such a good thing because you have to expend a great deal of effort to try to take full advantage of that float. Slip up by paying too soon and you've lost that opportunity gain.

You also have to pay by check to gain the extra use of the funds represented by your disbursement float, and this puts added pressure on your daily cash position management because it creates uncertainty about when the checks will clear back against your account. Think how much easier it would be if you paid electronically and could know exactly when the payments would be made instead of anticipating when checks would clear back against your account. Paying electronically also eliminates a number of "pesky" bank service changes associated with check payment, so your monthly bank charges are likely to be reduced if you can switch all or most of your payments to an electronic medium and eliminate the paper.

Why is float important?

Float is the delayed use of funds. It can work for or against a company. Float in disbursements works for a company by extending the time between sending a payment and its ultimate funding in a company's disbursement (bank) account. Float in collections works against a company by increasing the time before a company receives a payment, deposits the payment in its bank, and is able to use the funds.

Over the years, the importance of float has been tied to the rise and fall of interest rates and the resultant cost of funds for the corporation. There is no float with electronic payments, so the long-term outlook is for float to disappear as an issue. However, as checks are still the preferred —and the largest—payment mechanism, it is imperative that cash managers know how float affects their cash levels.

What does your worksheet look like without checks?

Would getting rid of checks, or getting rid of most of them, simplify things? Exhibit 5.3 shows the same data as in Exhibit 5.2 except for items that were check-related. Note that staff deposits are the only items that are checks, but these are deposited electronically using remote capture and deposit. Their value is not really significant, and leaving it on the worksheet is probably acceptable.

Exhibit 5.3 Worksheet with No Checks

Time Period/Week of: xx/xx/xx		{Date}		{Date}
($ millions)		Current Day		
	Estimate	Actual	Variance (act-est)	Estimate
Receipts/Inflows				
Beginning Balance	25,125	22,150	(2,975)	5,003
Staff deposits (rem.capt)	1,500	1,052	(448)	1,250
Maturing investments	10,000	10,555	555	15,000
Customer ACH payments	12,000	11,076	(924)	14,000
Miscellaneous cash inflows	1,000	975	(25)	2,000
International wires	8,000	5,625	(2,375)	10,000
TOTRECEIPTS/INFLOWS	57,625	51,433	(6,192)	47,253
Disbursements/Outflows			Variance (est-act)	
Target Cash Balances	2,000	2,250	(250)	4,500
Controlled disbursements	7,500	8,545	(1,045)	6,000
Payroll: direct deposit	20,650	20,360	290	2,500
ST debt maturing	1,520	1,875	(355)	5,000
LT debt repayment	0	0	0	6,000
Miscellaneous cash outflows	2,500	3,400	(900)	3,500
Wires	8,750	10,000	(1,250)	6,500
TOT DISBMTS/OUTFLOWS	42,920	46,430	(3,510)	34,000
NET CASH FLOW/Ending Bal.	**14,705**	**5,003**	**(9,702)**	**13,253**

As you can see the worksheet is not substantially reduced in number of entries. Eliminating the lockboxes simplified the inflows, while eliminating controlled disbursement clearings and payroll check clearings reduced the outflow items slightly. There is one bigger improvement than the reduction in number of items. With electronic payments (in and out) the estimates become more precise. You cannot see that directly from the exhibits, but considering that you do not have to anticipate when checks will clear or when customers checks will show up in a lockbox, you have better knowledge of your cash flows. This is very useful in managing the cash position.

6

Harnessing Cash Flows

Focusing on your cash position also means managing cash flows. You can have many types of payments associated with your business lines, transaction processing, mix of trading partners (e.g., corporate vs. consumer), and global locations. Making and receiving payments also create other transactions that you must handle in managing your cash position. These include concentration of deposits and funding of bank accounts to cover disbursements for payables, payroll, and taxes.

What types of payments can you expect? Exhibit 6.1 on the next page shows examples of the types of payments among the main paying and receiving groups—individuals (consumers), companies, government units, and banks. Your experience may differ somewhat, but this is a good general guide.

In the past, most of the payments shown in the exhibit have been paid by issuing and mailing checks. Today, it is possible to automate most of the payment types shown. This neatly deflates the paper-based float and makes estimating payment timing possible. It is easy to see that the more you can move your payments—and your customers' payments—into an electronic medium, the better off you'll be in managing your cash position.

Exhibit 6.1 Types of Payments

From \ To	Consumer	Business	Government	Bank
Consumer	• Gifts • Reimbursements • Loans	• Point of sale (POS) or purchase (POP) • Bill payment	• Tax payments • User fees	• Security purchases • Insurance premiums • Investment svcs • Deposits
Business	• Salaries • Expense reimbursements • Dividends • Purchase rebates	• Purchases of inventory, etc. • Utilities • Transportation expenses	• Tax payments • Licensing fees	• Pension paymts • Insurance premiums • Investment svcs • Loan repaymts • Service charges
Government	• Entitlements • Tax refunds	• Vendor payments • Tax refunds	• Federal to state funds transfers	• Vendor payments • Tax refunds
Bank	• Dividends • Mutual Fund redemptions • Insurance claims	• ST loans (lines) • Matured investments • Other services	• Securities trading • Taxes	• Security purchases • Wire transfers

What's Involved?

Handling payments efficiently is a major step in harnessing your cash flows. Newer techniques shorten or eliminate float delays commonly seen in old-time, paper-based systems. Making and receiving payments electronically—and this also includes using any card-based services, such as purchasing cards, streamlines your banking system significantly.

Being able to manage your cash position better usually means taking control over as much of the payment processes as you can practically. This really depends on your organizational structure and where the responsibilities for managing cash flows reside. This does not include the accounts receivable and accounts payable processing, but it usually means the end part of these processes—the payment part.

If you have a highly centralized system already, taking over the payments may not be difficult. However, if you have a heavily decentralized system, it may be harder to gain control over the payments. Fortunately, making payments electronically can help because there is no need for multiple bank relationships when you pay electronically. This means that you may not meet much resistance in gaining control over the payments.

What happens if you do not gain control over the payments? The first problem that you will face is a lack of accurate information until the last minute. This can prove costly in terms of higher borrowing rates or lower investment rates when you are forced to react quickly to an unplanned amount of payments. Usually, your inability to gain control will be affected by how autonomous the decentralized units have been, especially in terms of making payments.

Earlier, I commented on how people are able to cope with the most complicated, inefficient systems rather than change them. This is a similar situation. People do not like change, and your gaining control over payments that were previously made by a local financial manager will be hampered by "territorial battles." These may be extreme examples, but you should be prepared for them if your company is very decentralized.

Making Changes

If you are going to make changes to your current system, your first step should be to determine whether there is any documentation on the current system. If not, you'll have to develop it by interviewing key people who are now handling things. During these interviews you can also note the activities that cause the most problems or require the most time. From this you should have an excellent idea of what the new system needs to do.

Checks

A fact of life for all companies is dealing with checks. I have stated that I recommend eliminating as much of your check volume as possible. Much of the worry about fraud and the extra steps taken to ensure security over check issuance would not be necessary if everyone pushed to pay electronically. Of course, there are potential fraud situations with electronics too, but check fraud seems to be an institution in its own right.

There are a number of newer services that can help you in getting rid of the small, "nuisance" checks. They are discussed below in the card section.

Disbursements

One problem you may face in determining your cash needs is the dollar amount that will clear against disbursement accounts that day. Fortunately, there is a bank service that allows a cash manager to do just that—fund the company's disbursement accounts on the same day that the checks will be posted. The service is controlled disbursements. In the late morning, the company is notified via its bank's information reporting system of the dollar amount of checks that will be clearing against its accounts that same day. The company can then fund these accounts by wire transfer from another bank, by internal transfer within the same bank, or by having preauthorized an internal transfer from the same bank.

Banks are able to notify companies of the same-day checking amount because they receive the information from the Federal Reserve before it presents checks to them for payment. The banks, in turn, retransmit the information to individual customers via intraday reports available through the bank's information reporting system.

It is important that all of the clearing checks be presented through the Federal Reserve because the bank cannot identify other checks presented against the account, such as checks that are presented at a branch for payment. For this reason, banks use isolated branches or affiliated correspondent banks to process controlled disbursements because these locations will only receive checks for clearing from the Fed. To use the service, a company must move its disbursement accounts to the controlled disbursement location.

Instead of setting up one account for each disbursing location throughout the company, companies with smaller disbursement volume can arrange with their banks to use a high order sort or sub-account service. This identifies each location by a unique location code (usually the first three digits in the check number). The bank thus provides one controlled disbursement account that can be broken down by location for reconcilement purposes. This saves extra fees for individual accounts.

Bank reconciliation and positive pay services provide checks and balances over your bank accounts. Bank reconciliation services provide assurance that checks have been issued and cleared correctly. Positive pay services provide safeguards against check fraud, essentially serving as a daily account reconcilement. These two services are discussed further in Appendix C.

Card applications

Banks currently offer an increasing variety of card-based services that can greatly simplify making payments. In more recent times, banks have offered purchasing cards, or p-cards, which organizations issue to their employees for use in making purchases other than travel and entertainment (although there are now combination cards). Using p-cards for routine, small-dollar purchases, such as office supplies, greatly reduces check issuance and check processing costs. It also establishes better control over these activities and makes central funding once monthly possible.

Banks are also pushing card applications into the payables disbursements area. In this instance, the bank taps into its merchant data base to match up vendors that accept credit cards with companies who pay to that vendor currently by check. The bank solicits the vendor, and, if the vendor agrees, the company converts to paying the vendor via a card transaction. These payments settle monthly (or some other agreed-upon schedule) between the bank and the company, and the vendor gets paid by processing the company's bill like a credit card transaction. The bank usually offers to share its card commission with the company.

Banks have also expanded card services for other corporate payments. For payrolls for employees who do not have bank accounts or are part-time employees, such as at a university, banks can provide pay cards, which allow the recipient to draw cash from the bank's (or often any bank's) ATM instead of receiving a pay check. Governments have adopted pay cards for payments associated with welfare or food stamps. Pay cards work like a bank debit card. The bank has essentially created a bank account for the pay card recipient—just without the checks.

Card services help you manage the cash position more effectively because they reduce the number of transactions, consolidate data for better information reporting, and establish set transaction dates for better forecasting. Add to this possible cost savings in reduced check processing costs and revenue-sharing with the bank, and these services can be valuable ones.

Collections

In most cases, the best practice for collections involves the establishment of a system that accelerates payments as well as their information content, such as the customer's name and identification number and which invoices are being paid. This is needed to apply cash against the customers' accounts. From the collecting company's point of view, the way to achieve this best practice is to establish an electronic collection network. This can apply to either retail or wholesale companies.

Cash collections systems are a function of the types of customers a company has and the methods of payment customers use. For instance, if a company's sales are made at retail locations, it cannot take advantage of the benefits offered by bank lockbox services. It must deal with organizing and controlling local deposits and concentrating these deposits efficiently and economically. On the other hand, if a company manufactures and sells products to other businesses, it can use a bank lockbox service to expedite processing and clearing of check payments.

A typical network for a company will include both electronic and check payments. There is no "one size fits all" solution here as each company's environment is different. Checks from one type of customer are directed to a bank lockbox, while electronic payments from another type of customer are transmitted through the ACH system. You have to be prepared to adapt possible solutions to the way your organization works.

Improved Handling of Payments

Banks have been expanding their use of imaging technology to provide more information to their business customers. The primary services affected are lockbox, account reconciliation (check copies), and positive pay. By transmitting images of checks and remittance documents, lockbox services provide payment information much faster than they could previously. On the disbursements side, being able to retrieve copies of checks on-line or to inspect suspected forged checks caught by positive pay services, financial managers can make better decisions while they use bank services to protect their organizations' assets.

Converting checks to an electronic form is a recent technological development that has the potential to radically change how payments are processed. Consumer checks can be converted to ACH debits using the accounts receivable conversion (ARC) format, while business checks can be converted to electronic image replacement documents (IRDs).

Retail payments can be made by credit/debit cards or electronic checks (which are converted to ACH debits or digitized images) or by direct debit (ACH debits). Payments that can be processed through point of sale (POS) systems can clear electronically. Direct debit programs are used by companies to collect routine payments for services, such as utilities, telecommunications service providers, cable TV companies, and insurance companies, and credit card companies.

Wholesale payments can also be converted to electronic payments (instead of checks) by negotiations between trading partners (buyer and seller). To receive electronic payments, the seller might offer additional incentives, such as a discount or slightly longer payment terms, to the buyer. The buyer also can gain benefit by paying electronically since the costs for doing so are typically much less than paying by check, especially when interest rates are below their normal ranges.

New technology for handling checks

New technologies for handling checks deal with converting the paper checks into electronic formats or images, which can clear much faster. These new developments offer the potential to simplify collection systems. This technology can eliminate the need for elaborate concentration systems.

Exhibit 6.2 Remote Capture/Deposit

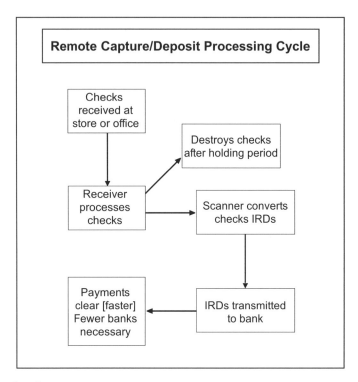

Check 21

In 2004, the U.S. Congress passed the Check Clearing for the 21st Century act. This new law has ushered in a new method for handling check deposits.

Exhibit 6.2 shows how a new service, remote capture/deposit works. With remote capture, checks are scanned at the location where they are received, such as a retail outlet, office, or even a bank branch. When scanned, the checks become digitized images, called image replacement documents (IRDs). These IRDs can be transmitted to any bank; they no longer have to be deposited in a local branch or re-mailed to a bank lockbox service. From the depositing company's point of view, this new service offers the op-

Impact of remote capture

It is expected that the services to be most impacted by remote capture are:

Check returns

Returned checks should be easier to re-present because electronic images can be re-transmitted much faster than physically sending a returned check back and forth through the payments system to re-clear.

Controlled disbursements

As checks clear faster through remote capture services, any extended float gained by using controlled disbursement accounts will be all but eliminated. Banks also will have to handle checks that are presented directly on the controlled disbursement location. Without a way to capture this information on a timely basis or limit check presentments to the early morning, banks may not be able to report the entire amount clearing that day, thus diminishing the value of controlled disbursement accounts.

Depository services

Banks will have to adapt their depository services to accommodate the new source of check deposits. Many users of remote capture services will naturally expect to share in any cost savings that are created by using this new service.

Lockbox

Banks may see decreased lockbox activity as marginal lockbox customers switch to remote capture rather than maintain a lockbox. Organizations with moderate volumes may find it cost-effective to simply scan and transmit checks in much less time and effort than directing payments to a lockbox.

Check images

Companies will have to get used to using check images instead of actual checks or photocopies.

portunity to greatly reduce local banking activity and further consolidate banking services.

If wholesale payments cannot be converted to electronic payments, then the "next" best practice is to use a bank lockbox service. Although not as desirable as an electronic payment, it is much better than receiving the checks at a company location and depositing them in a bank branch. This latter activity may not be too costly for retail deposits, but it is uneconomical for wholesale payments. An acceptable bank lockbox arrangement is one in which the checks deposited today are available tomorrow or the next business day. This one-day availability lays the groundwork for best practices in cash concentration.

Other new technology for lockbox

One newer development in bank lockbox services is converting checks received in a lockbox to an electronic form. This electronic format for the converted check is the Accounts Receivable Check (ARC) format. Its initial target has been retail (consumer) checks. Corporate checks cannot be converted without new legislation permitting it, such as Check 21.

In addition to ARC conversion, which essentially "truncates" the check when it is received in the lockbox processing area, banks offer imaging services, which transmit images of the checks received to companies daily. This is not restricted to ARC conversions as there are no legal barriers to sending images of business checks.

The technology to convert or eliminate paper in lockbox processing is still in an early stage of development. However, as its acceptance and adoption grow, it can reduce the paperwork headaches and delays commonly found in today's systems. It should also reduce the handling needed in lockbox processing, which could result in lower prices.

Mobilizing Funds

Funds should be dynamic, not static. This means that you want to build your cash management system so that your funds move with as little manual intervention as possible, especially funds that are being concentrated. In this way, funds will move rapidly and efficiently to the proper place to be used in managing the cash position.

Concentration of funds

Cash concentration usually refers to mobilizing funds from multiple company banks (not branches of the same bank) to one main bank. The purpose is to have all the company funds in one location. The concentration account is sometimes referred to as a company's operating account, funding account, or general account. Nevertheless, they all refer to the master account where the company's funds are domiciled.

Companies with bank accounts in multiple banks in the same or different geographic areas normally aggregate all their corporate funds from all banks into one concentration account for the purpose of efficiency and effectiveness. A company that has only one bank relationship, with all its banking conducted at that bank and its branches, can easily mobilize its funds.

Interstate banking, which has experienced the growth of widespread coverage by the largest banks, can help reduce the number of banks used with local deposit systems. When coupled with new technology like Check 21, companies do not have to maintain collection and concentration systems containing dozens of banks.

The concentration account is used to receive incoming funds from internal book transfers at the same bank, from other accounts (e.g., lockbox accounts), incoming wires from other lockbox banks, incoming ACHs from customers or from depository banks, incoming wires from other banks or customers, and over-the-counter check deposits.

The concentration account is typically used to fund controlled disbursement and zero-balance disbursement accounts, to fund the payroll accounts, to pay federal and state government taxes, to pay off loans, and to fund investments.

There are two main ways to concentrate funds: wire transfer and the ACH. With wires, the company checks its balances periodically, preferably daily, to determine there are funds available to be moved from the depository bank. (Note that only the available or the collected balance is eligible to be transferred.) If there are sufficient funds to be transferred, the company initiates a wire

Exhibit 6.3 Concentrating Receipts

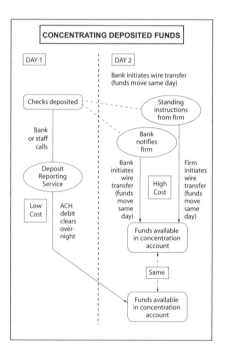

transfer (usually via PC) from the depository account to its concentration account. As an alternative, the company could arrange
to have its depository bank review the account balance daily and
to wire out any available (same-day) funds over a predetermined
target level. These arrangements are shown on the left-hand side
of Exhibit 6.3.

However, the wire transfer arrangement shown in the exhibit is prone to error. The company cash manager or the bank
staff person may fail to check the balance in the receipt account
each day. Another problem arises when there is heavy activity

and not enough time for either cash manager or banker to check balances and make a transfer. The final shortcoming of this approach is the relative high cost of wire transfers.

For bank lockbox concentration, assuming that the checks clear in one business day on average, the concentration technique of choice is the ACH transfer method. In this method, bank lockbox personnel call in the deposit via a reporting service or directly to the concentration bank. The concentration bank creates an ACH debit that clears overnight, giving the company available (collected or "good" funds) in its concentration account. This system can be set up to run with or without intervention by the company's cash manager. In most cases, the best practice does not involve any intervention.

Using the ACH for concentration eliminates some of the problems with wire transfers. With ACH, deposit locations (such as a lockbox department or local store) call in the daily deposits to a deposit reporting service on the same day the deposit is made. This can be a weakness as locations may neglect to report a deposit on time or even understand the importance of regular daily deposits. As a result you need a report to monitor the deposit activity. Your concentration bank can provide this late in the same business day that the deposits are supposed to be made. It is usually available under same-day reporting services. With this report you can spot missing deposits and rectify the situation quickly. This should be part of your daily routine. The deposit reporting service, a third party or the concentration bank, initiates the ACH transaction that transfers the daily deposit overnight to the concentration bank.

There are specific circumstances where intervention can be acceptable. Examples are large retailers or fast food chains that have to deposit substantial amounts of cash daily or that have a lot of business activity on the weekends. To move funds in these situations, the company's cash manager creates an anticipatory ACH transfer, which is a transfer for most, but not all, of the expected (or *anticipated*) deposit before the deposit is made so that the ACH debit and currency deposit arrive at the same time. To be safe, the transfers are usually for a percentage of the anticipated amount, depending on how accurate and reliable the cash forecasts have been.

ACH transfers offer distinct advantages to companies that use them for concentration of funds. First, they are substantially cheaper than using the alternative—wire transfer. In addition, they are reliable in that the transfer can be made part of a routine that can be performed daily without exception. Even small payments that would not be economical to transfer out by wire can be transferred economically by ACH. Finally, an ACH system is flexible, able to add or delete deposit locations easily.

ACH transfer systems are also the best practice for concentrating funds from retail locations. This system works in the same manner as discussed above except that the company's employees are the parties reporting the deposits to the concentration bank.

In some cases, such as where a bank's branches can be matched with most or all of a company's retail points, a company can use the bank's branch location system to concentrate funds into one central account. This service is called deposit reconciliation or deposit concentration.

Wire transfers should not be used to concentrate funds except in special conditions. For example a wire can be used as an exception when an ACH reporting location has failed to report a deposit and a day has elapsed. The funds can still be transferred via wire on the same day, so no availability is lost. However, there is a higher bank charge.

Wires can also be used if there is a substantial amount of same-day funds available in a depository bank. A cash manager can discover this from the daily bank balance and information reporting system. If the amount of funds available today has come from today's deposits, it may be a better choice to use wires.

For lockboxes and local store deposits, most checks will clear in approximately one business day. Even if some checks take an additional day to clear, their dollar amount is often equal to or exceeded by the dollar amount of same-day checks. These amounts then offset, resulting in a net one-day clearance float. With the net one-day clearance, the concentration initiator (the bank or cash manager) can safely initiate an ACH debit transaction to draw the funds out of the depository account and move them to the company's concentration account.

By obtaining this information on the day of the deposit, the cash manager can compute the dollars that will be available the following day (the amounts of zero or same-day and one-day funds) and initiate the ACH debit to concentrate these funds overnight. This approach loses the use of the same-day funds for one day, but, unless this amount is significant, it still offers a very low-cost concentration system.

An alternative to using the ACH to concentrate funds is using a *zero balance account* (ZBA) arrangement with a bank that has branches that match up with a company's depositing locations. Stores make local deposits into a ZBA sub-account, and all deposits are cleared automatically to a single master account. For significantly large amounts, wires are usually used daily. Since the cash manager has to review the balances daily anyway, initiating a wire transfer on days when large amounts of same-day funds are available is easy to do. A way of calculating the cost benefit of using wires vs. the ACH is shown below. The downside with this approach is that it still requires intervention by the cash manager.

As I mentioned previously, one method that eliminates concentration headaches is to develop a one-bank system so that your deposits are concentrated through the bank's own system. In this case you still may have to install a monitoring system to assure that deposits are being made. Fortunately, most cash management banks can help you with this.

Exhibit 6.4 Comparing Concentration Methods

Method	*Advantages*	*Disadvantages*	*Cost*
Wire transfer	Same-day value	Expensive; requires action by cash manager or bank	Approximately $20 per wire
ACH	Inexpensive; can be set up to operate with little or no intervention	Cannot transfer funds for same-day value easily	Approximately $1 per transfer
ZBA	Simple; all transactions within same bank	Restricted to same bank	Cost of ZBA account(s)

Comparing concentration methods and costs

The various methods for concentrating funds—wire transfer, ACH, and ZBA—are shown in Exhibit 6.4 on the preceding page. The exhibit shows the advantages, disadvantages, and costs for each method. The method used depends on a number of factors. Perhaps the most important factors are the time it will take the concentrated funds to become available funds and their magnitude.

Below is an illustration of how you compute whether to use a wire transfer or the ACH to concentrate funds.

Comparing Concentration Costs: Wires vs. ACH

What return is needed to justify using a wire when a wire transfer costs \$20 and a transfer using the ACH costs \$1?

Assume an internal rate of return of 7% and a pick up of one business day:

$$\$X = (20\text{-}1) / (.07/365)$$
$$\$X = (19) / (.0001917) = \$99,113$$

If the amount of immediately available funds equals or exceeds \$99,113, it justifies making a wire transfer. If it is less, then the ACH should be used.

Systems and Treasury Work Stations

Many larger firms consider using treasury work stations, while smaller to- mid-sized firms count on their bank information reporting systems for substantial decision support in managing cash management operations. Most work stations are provided by non-bank software firms. Major providers of treasury management systems include Gateway, Kyriba, Sungard, Thomson, Trema, and XRT-CERG.

It is getting harder to determine the difference between a treasury work station and a bank information reporting system. They have many features that are similar, if not identical. Exhibit

6.5 offers a comparison of the two types of systems, showing which features are standard in most instances and those that are customized items or are not offered. In addition to the features shown, a treasury work station usually has strong data integration and data base management features. These are usually far more advanced and can handle more than one bank, and this clearly differentiates them from most, if not all, bank information reporting services. This does not mean that the "gap" between the two types will remain. Information systems have been dramatically improved in recent times, so it is logical to expect that they will continue to offer attractive new features. For corporations with simpler data requirements, they represent useful, cost-effective treasury system tools.

Defining treasury system requirements also means detailing what's in a treasury management system or can be provided by a treasury work station. Usually the following pieces are included:

- **System communications**: Tools to manage overall system data bases, handle communications with banks and/or other organizations (e.g., auto-dial capabilities, file parsing utilities).

- **Bank information reporting**: Interface with all bank reporting systems, incorporating bank reports into master data base.

- **Cash position management**: Programs to record daily bank balances, funds transfers, and target balances, usually in the form of a cash worksheet.

- **Specific applications or "core" modules:** A typical work station includes modules such as: treasury-accounting reporting, short-term liquidity management (both investing and borrowing), cash forecasting (templates), banking relations documentation

- **Additional applications (not part of core modules):** A work station provider can add specific extra modules, such as foreign exchange (FX) management and trading, letter of credit initiation and processing, and long-term liquidity management.

- **Data integration capabilities**: with off-the-shelf software to avoid reentering data (and transforming the data for spreadsheet use automatically).

  Special analytical tools: report writer, file management, automatic communications (beyond bank links).

Exhibit 6.5
Treasury Work Stations vs. Bank Information Systems

Features	Treas. Work Station	Bank Info. Services
System communications	Standard	Standard
Bank balances & details	Standard	Only for same bank
Multibank reporting	Standard	Separate service
Cash position mgmt.	Standard	Only in some
Bank relationship mgmt.	Standard	Rarely included
Funds transfer capability	Standard	Only for same bank
Treasury-accounting link	Standard	Not included
Short-term investments	Standard	Some (not inmost)
Short-term debt	Standard	Rarely included
Cash forecasting	Standard	Not included
Foreign exchange trading/reporting	May be separate	Not included
Data integration capabilities	Standard	Only in some
Ease of implementation	Moderate to complex	Easy for MS Windows
Level of technical support	High in most	Minimal
Costs	Substantial for most	Moderate, but could mount up

Using More Electronics

As I have mentioned previously, it pays to be as electronic as you can. The benefits in better information, lower costs, simpler systems, and more reliable forecasts are just too attractive to ignore. Once you have adjusted to losing float, you should really appreciate the power of electronic payments.

How do you get trading partners—customers and suppliers—to convert from paper-based checks to electronic payments? This takes a concerted effort and a good deal of time. Companies that have been successful in converting major trading partners have started with their largest ones and worked down to the smallest ones. They also had everyone who is affected by payments aboard on the program to convert to electronic payments. For smaller businesses, it may be difficult to convince large trading partners to switch from paper to electronic.

Domestic electronic payment systems

Electronic transactions do not rely on paper to move money. There are two types of electronic transfers in the U.S. banking system: (1) wire transfers using the Federal Reserve's Fed wire system and (2) Automated Clearing House (ACH) items. Both methods are referred to as electronic funds transfer (EFT) transactions. EFT is the transmission of an electronic message to a depository financial institution requesting that funds be transferred from one account to another account with another bank.

Fedwire

Fedwire is the most important domestic (U.S.) payments system. When we say "wire transfers," we mean Fedwire. It is used for large-dollar transfers, and much of its volume comes from large transfers among participants in the financial markets and among banks throughout the country. The designated receiver is guaranteed the funds by the Federal Reserve, which stands behind Fedwire funds transfers, ready to make up any shortfalls.

Companies use Fedwire when they need the assurance that the transfer has been made. For example, the parties involved in the sale of an operating unit rely on Fedwire and the reference number for the transfer—which indicates that the transfer went through—to complete the deal. Companies also use Fedwire when they make investments, move funds to another bank to fund the bank accounts, and move large amounts of funds from deposit banks.

Fedwire transfers settle through the Federal Reserve Bank. These are real-time transactions in which the Federal Reserve accounts of the payee and payor financial institutions are simultaneously settled. Immediately upon receiving instructions from the payor institution, the Fed reduces the payor's account and increases the payee account by a like amount. Once the Federal Reserve Bank books the debit and credit entry that transfers value, the transaction is irrevocable. Each completed transfer is assigned a Fedwire number by which the payment can be traced to the payee's account and confirmed. Wire transfers are the most expensive method of payment. For that reason, they are typically used only when a company requires an immediate and final settlement of funds, such as in a purchase of real estate.

ACH Funds Movement

For smaller amounts, such as direct deposit of payroll, state, local, and federal tax payments, and pension and retirement payments, companies access the ACH through their banks. The ACH is also used for payment settlement in point-of-sale (POS) systems. POS systems transfer payment information to charge a cardholder's account (for a credit card) or debit a cardholder's account (for a debit card). The ACH is then used to transfer funds to the merchant's (company's) bank account.

The ACH's role in overall payments is growing, and good cash management systems use it as much as possible because it is reliable and inexpensive when compared to other payment alternatives.

Automated Clearing House (ACH) transactions operate according to rules and guidelines promulgated by the not-for-profit National Automated Clearing House Association (NACHA). ACH transactions are most widely known as the means by which direct deposit payroll is settled. ACH payments may, however, be set up to either debit or credit the originating company's account. For this reason, the terms "payee" and "payor" are not used in describing ACH transactions. The parties instead are referred to as the "originator" or the "recipient" and a transaction is described as either an "ACH credit" or an "ACH debit." ACH credit transactions move funds from the originator's account to the receiver's account while ACH debit transactions move funds from the receiver's account to the originator's account. For example, with a direct deposit payroll transaction, the "originator" is the employer, the "recipient" is the employee and the transaction type is an "ACH credit." In the instance of a utility company collecting payments on a monthly basis from its customers, the utility company is again the "originator," the customer is the "recipient" but the transaction type is an "ACH debit."

A company may initiate a single ACH transaction, but typically the ACH process is used as a batch process permitting thousands of ACH transactions to occur at the same time at a low cost per transaction. As a batch process, ACH transactions do not settle immediately and simultaneously as Fedwire transfers do. ACH credit transfers for payroll direct deposit, for example, must be originated at least two business days prior to the settlement (value) date. Under NACHA guidelines, there are specified circumstances that permit the return of the ACH debits and credits. Unlike Fed wire transactions, payments made through the ACH network are neither immediately settled nor irrevocable.

7

The Need for Accurate Cash Flow Forecasts

As I have mentioned in other chapters, accurate cash flow forecasts are the backbone of sound cash management in general and of cash position management specifically. You cannot afford to do this poorly; if you do, you will pay for it in extra time consumed and additional costs associated with making too many decisions without sufficient lead time.

Your forecasting should be structured using the factors and timing shown in Exhibit 7.1 on the next page. Note that the recommended format for all three types of short-term forecasts is the same—receipts and disbursements. You do not want to confuse your forecasts with input from financial statements, accounting reports, and budget reports or systems. Keep the terminology in cash flow terms—e.g., disbursements, not payables and collections, not receivables.

I don't mean that you should ignore financial statements and other reports. If you use them, you will have to translate them into terms (and flows) that you can manage.

All three types of forecast should be maintained on a rolling basis for the time periods shown in the exhibit. Since your business continues on a rolling basis, so should your forecasts.

Exhibit 7.1 Cash Flow Forecasting Systems

	Daily	**Short Term**	**Longer Term**
Time Horizon	Daily for next 10 business days	Weekly for next 4-6 weeks	Monthly for next 12 months
Format	Receipts & Disbursements	Receipts & Disbursements	Receipts & Disbursements
Techniques	Simple projections	Simple projections	Projection models and averages
Accuracy	Very high	High	Moderate
Reliability	Very high	High	Fairly high
Uses	Daily cash management	Planning week to week	Planning month to month

Overlapping the time periods for your forecasts may give you insight into possible errors in any one. If you can match your rolling 4-6 week forecast with the first month of you rolling 12-month forecast, you can see whether they are aligning or not. Similarly, you can look at the full 5 days with the first week of the rolling 4-to-6-week forecast. Of course, timing differences may throw things off somewhat, but you are really looking for major discrepancies as a warning signal.

Another good technique is to separate operating and financial cash flows. Financial flows may be easier to estimate because of the "rollover effect." When you are a constant investor or borrower, you will tend to settle into a consistent level of activity, rolling over investments or loans routinely. If this is the case, then you may be able to establish a minimum level of financial activity from which you can start on every business day. You are really interested in the net operating cash, so segregating should simplify your forecasting challenge. In fact, operating cash flows may often net out to zero, making the estimate of the financial flows the critical element of your forecast. What you will need to know are lead times for initiating or decreasing the levels of financial flows.

If you have been involved with short- and medium-term cash flow forecasting at all, you realize that little scientific and mathematical skills are needed. Experience with the numbers, trends, seasonal shifts, and data sources will outweigh a statistical skill set.

The most common approach to cash flow forecasting probably is consolidating estimates obtained from "knowledgeable" sources. These numbers may be modified, but in most cases they are not.

Cash flow forecasts can often be tailored to meet the company's needs by spreading out payments or enforcing payment terms more rigorously. Timing investment or debt maturities also can even out cash flows. If you only knew then what you know now, forecasting would be a breeze.

If your daily forecast is inaccurate, you will face major surprises when cash flows do not occur as predicted. You can live with the occasional slippage in the daily forecast, but if it is a continuing problem, you will stop relying on it and will tend to react to information only as it becomes available. This short lead time exposes your organization to sudden rate changes or other undesirable circumstances, so you want to do everything you can to make the daily cash forecast a reliable tool.

You should expect the daily forecast to be very accurate because many of the data items are really known. It's really their *timing* that you are trying to determine. Perhaps calling it a *forecast* is not a proper description. You are really scheduling the known cash flows over the short-term horizon and estimating when the other cash flows will likely occur (maybe they should be called "not completely known"). In most cases, your daily cash forecast or schedule should be accurate and easy to work with. If it is not, then you probably need to analyze the entire system for gathering and assimilating daily cash flow estimates and make any necessary revisions to the current procedures.

Ideally, you want to obtain as much visibility into expected cash flows as possible. However, it may be difficult for your sources to estimate farther out than 30-60 days with a high degree of accuracy. You should still collect the data if for no other reason than using it to build a historical data base with which you can develop other predictive models.

Rolling Daily Forecast

The format of the daily forecast should be a day-to-day maturity schedule over the next 1-2 weeks. If you have data farther out in the future, you can track it with a collective maturity schedule. An example of a maturity schedule is shown in Exhibit 7.2. This has been modified for the illustration, but it extends out as far as necessary to include all known short-term investment and borrowing maturities. The "Days" column has been adjusted to fit into the 1-5 range. Obviously, you would probably be looking out farther, and this would be easy to do in a spreadsheet.

On the exhibit, securities are aggregated by type—i.e., investment or borrowing security—and are then recorded, noting the details asked for in each first four columns. Once the amount, rate, and days to maturity are entered for a security item, the maturity date can be scheduled. You probably do not have to worry about weekend maturity dates if you are using a simple projection of the security's maturity date because the maturity date is typically confirmed at the time the transaction is completed.

Entries for all types of securities are entered and are "aged" into the proper maturity date. Each maturity date can then be totaled and fed into the daily cash forecast. The net number for any date is an important number, but so are the individual maturities because you still have to handle those transactions. This means that the maturity schedule may come to resemble the daily cash worksheet.

Benefits of good forecasting

Even companies that do not experience cash crises can enjoy significant benefits by formalizing and periodically refining the forecasting process. There are real benefits to having a good forecasting process. Not all are quantifiable in dollar terms. The benefits are shown in Exhibit 7.3.

A good forecast makes your life easier. It provides a reliable guide for your financial activities, both in the short and longer

Exhibit 7.2 Illustration of a Maturity Schedule

				Maturity Dates (from current)					
Security	*Amt*	*Rate*	*Days*	*0*	*1*	*2*	*3*	*4*	*5*
Inv. Type	($000)		5						
Bank CD	10,000	3.45%	3						10,000
Corp CD	15,000	3.38%					15,000		
Debt Type									
Bank loan	5,000	5.65%	5						(5,000)
CP	25,000	4.35%	3				(25,000)		
Net Maturity							(10,000)		5,000

term. Without it, you face a complex environment without any support beyond a few days. You exist in a virtual reactive world, waiting for events to happen and then responding. Contrast this with the proactive financial manager who anticipates major needs and can invest with the assurance that the funds will not be needed before maturity.

If your forecast is reasonably accurate, you can be a better shopper for short-term investments or an informed borrower, able to time your loans to mature just as you receive funds. This means that you are able to use your short-term borrowing facilities efficiently and save the costs of excessive credit facilities that you do not need. It also means that you can titrate your borrowings, reducing your interest expense.

Treasury management is not much fun without a good forecast. Finance is as essential to a firm's success as is production, marketing, and other areas. Just as plans are needed for other operating areas to function properly, so it is with finance.

Exhibit 7.3 Benefits of Good Forecasting

The benefits of good forecasting include:

1. **Avoiding bad financing decisions.**
   One costly pitfall that can be avoided through a good cash forecast is the forced reversal of a previous financing decision.

2. **Investing in higher-yielding instruments.**
   A good cash forecast will allow treasury staff to invest funds for a longer period of time, rather than keep precautionary balances or invest only in lower-yielding overnight alternatives.

3. **Investing earlier each day.**
   This improvement may be a significant advantage for investment or borrowing decisions because the best rates are usually available in the morning.

4. **Increased staff productivity.**
   Duplicating efforts can be eliminated with a centrally coordinated cash forecast.

5. **Increased credibility.**
   In repeated surveys, CEOs indicate that they value treasury *most* for its ability to manage liquidity and provide reliable cash forecasts. The benefit could be as great as saving the company's very existence, but in any case, it gives management more time to react. Other stakeholders, such as bank lenders, place a premium on good cash forecasts and measure management's credibility by it.

6. **Improved intra-company communication.**
   The process, as well as the end product, helps develop better, more proactive interdepartmental relationships. It forces a coordination of outbound and inbound flows, so that purchasing, accounts payable, accounts receivable, and collections are all brought into a single conversation.

Effects of poor forecasting

Low reliability means more guesswork. If you cannot forecast your cash flows effectively, a number of unfavorable consequences are likely.

If you are uncertain when you will need funds or even have excess funds to invest, you borrow or invest for short periods of time and spend more time making frequent loans or investments. Furthermore, you probably lose any benefits you might derive from longer maturities, such as lower borrowing rates and more attractive yields on your investments.

If you are unsure about your needs, you constantly maintain high liquidity, usually in the form of safe investments like U.S. t-bills or large amounts of bank credit lines or commercial paper programs. These can be costly since you will either lose investment yields or will increase your debt costs from compensating your banks for the credit lines or paying your dealer to sell your commercial paper.

Similar to short maturities, constantly rolling over investment or loans usually means increased costs. When you continually roll over, you tend to focus more on the rolling over and less on other details, such as the rate or at rates for other maturities. As a result, your costs increase.

Poor forecasts create more reactive situations, which usually result in making investment or borrowing decisions on the fly. As a result, you may end up borrowing on a day when you receive some unexpected receipts, or, conversely, investing funds that are needed to handle an unexpected disbursement. In most cases, you will have to borrow at a higher rate than you can comfortably invest any excess funds. This differential, over time, can be costly.

If you stay short with investments or borrowings, you may be able to handle the uncertainties in your forecast, but you then are susceptible to changes in short-term investment or borrowing rates. You lose the ability to spread out maturities so that any one day does not create a problem rate-wise. You also lose the ability to invest out farther to take advantages of better yields.

The overall result from ineffective forecasts is a higher cost for your working capital. Inefficient use of credit lines and lost interest income can mount up over time and become a drain on the company's overall liquidity and profitability positions.

Why Your Forecasting System Is Different

To undertake cash forecasting, you must first develop an understanding of your firm. Here are a few questions to get you started:

Where are the major sales-generating locations?

Are they decentralized, regional, or centralized? Your forecasting system may depend on information from the most knowledgeable sources, and these sources are usually near the sales location. In other words, the first step is to build your forecast so that it reflects your organization. One of the most common errors in forecasting is trying to complete a forecast that is not anything like the organization's structure.

Is your forecasting system tied into budgeting?

If so, you could be in trouble. Budgets can be effective management tools, but they really have nothing to do with a cash flow forecasting system. You want to encourage the sources for your forecasting data to give you the clearest picture of what they think is likely to happen. If the budget looms, your forecast data will be more likely to conform to the budget, not to what your sources expect to happen. You don't want this to happen.

Do you have good contacts at each operating location?

In addition to identifying the best sources, you need reliable, friendly sources at each operating location or department. Nurturing these sources takes time and effort, but the rewards are satisfying if you get a good forecasting system out of it.

Can you independently confirm local estimates?

Although you may have set up a good system, you should not rely on the network to provide all the data, especially the actual information. Use your sources for the estimates, but develop independent means of gathering the actual numbers.

How are payments received and made?

Do you have any control over them? Ideally, you should have a great deal of influence over receipt and payment locations, so you can try to construct an efficient cash management processing system that can provide good cash control and can spin off data necessary for regular forecasting. In this manner you may be able to get actual data independently.

Where are capital budget decisions made?

Who tracks how much has been spent and how much is still to be spent? Are capital expenditures substantial? Are they locked in once approved—i.e., are they ever aborted, thus freeing up claims on cash? Capital budgeting payments can foul up your forecast with "surprise" payments that could have been handled smoothly with lead time.

How much does the company invest and/or borrow?

In the short term? In the longer term (if at all)? Are maturity schedules maintained? How far out do these schedules go? It's easy sometimes to forget your financial activity, but these activities are often very critical factors in determining the organization's short-term liquidity position. If your liquidity management function is extremely active, you will need to develop a forecast of investing or borrowing levels to tie into your operational cash flows. Maintaining historical data on liquidity levels is an important ingredient in an efficient forecasting system.

Is treasury plugged in to merger and acquisition activities? Does this include spin-offs?

These tend to be big transactions with long lead times, but the effects on a forecast can be serious if treasury is not informed until the last moment.

Relevance and focus

Sometimes it can be confusing as to which cash flows are *relevant*. If you have a simple organization in which all operations are included in one comprehensive accounting system, inter-divisional cash flows can be netted without moving funds. As long as none of these inter-divisional flows are included in your forecasting system, your forecasting task should be much easier. However, this is not the case for many firms. Many subsidiaries manage their own funds and have limited funds flows with the parent. On the other hand, some subsidiaries have "outsourced" their treasury management activity to the parent, so their flows might be treated as a divisional flow.

This raises the subject of *focus*. You need to establish a proper focal point for your forecasting system. You should be focusing on cash flows into and from your point of view, which is the parent's viewpoint not that of a major subsidiary. If a sub is relatively independent and only interacts with your point when it needs funds or has excess funds, both of which trigger actions within a borrowing/investing agreement between the parent and sub, then that flow, which represents an increase or decrease to the subsidiary's "balance" with the parent, is the one you need to forecast. Although this need or excess may be derived from the sub's cash flows, you don't need to forecast those flows. You want to focus on the flows between the sub and the parent. Other typical flows might include tax payments and dividend payments, so you don't want to overlook them.

You need to decide first how important it is to "get it right." If you are lucky enough to have a steady flow of revenue that exceeds your outflow, then your forecast will have to be sensitive to maximizing the time that funds can be invested before they are needed for operations or to fuel the organization's growth. This does not mean that you can get by with weak or no forecasting. It means that you will forego upside gains if you do a poor job in forecasting. In any case, a bad forecast is something that you can use a base for developing a new system. It is often easier to improve the existing system than to create something that is brand new.

Forecasting in Smaller Companies

In a small company, the forecast tends to be in the head of the company's senior executive or executives. As the company grows, an in-the-head forecast is insufficient and risky. The leader's vision has to be transmitted to those who manage the various functions of the company.

As the company continues to grow, senior leaders need to know if planned growth can be financed successfully. A solid forecasting system allows this to happen.

Seasonality and Other Effects on Cash Levels

Many companies face predictable peaks and valleys in their business throughout the year. For instance, manufacturers of consumer electronics products get the bulk of their sales in the Christmas shopping season (from late November through the end of the year). This means that they have build-up of products that are shipped well before they receive payment. Thus, they have to finance this inventory roll-out before they receive any cash. During this period, they are likely to use up most or all of the temporary excess funds they set aside or to tap into the credit lines they arranged for this purpose. When sales roll in during the busy shopping season, they use the proceeds to pay down the borrowing and then invest any excess.

Other factors influencing a company's cash needs may be associated with non-operating activities, such as major capital expenditure programs, mergers and acquisitions, sales or disposition of company assets, as well as the timing of long-term financial transactions, such as bond issues, private placements of debt or equity, and equity issues. Any of these activities can create a temporary situation in which the company's normal cash flows are greatly modified. Since many of them are known with some lead time, it is usually possible to factor in the flows with the rolling daily/weekly cash flow forecast. Otherwise, the non-operating flows will come as a pleasant or unpleasant surprise.

Predicting the peak need caused by seasonality or other non-operating activities is important if the company must borrow funds to cover the need. It is important to remember that the *peak* need (i.e., not the average) must be covered, so facilities to handle it must be in place beforehand. If a company sets aside too much, it will incur excess costs that are unjustified. If it sets aside too little, it will have to pay a penalty to raise funds quickly. In either case, it is a costly error. A reliable forecast helps avoid this situation.

Maintaining History

You need to maintain, retain, and edit historical information about cash flows and related items. This is needed for current operations, expanded operations, and acquired operations. You need an overall view as well as one for each forecasting entity.

What are you looking for? Several things, including:

- Patterns—Is there seasonality? Are there any volume trends?

- Directions—What are signs (positive or negative) of net cash flows for each forecasting period?

- Tracking – Is a given period tracking against the same period in history? Why or why not?

- How did a historical event, such as a major financial transaction, or physical disaster, affect net cash flows? Use historical effects to customize current/new forecasts. Don't require or ask your forecast sources to do this.

- How have forecast sources done in the recent past? Should you keep a scorecard?

- Were there any special effects—geographic, global, or industrial—over time? If so, record them for possible use at a future time.

Above all, learn from history.

Reliable Sources

You are probably not going to be in a position to be able to do all the forecasting yourself. You will be dependent on others for estimates of cash flow items or for estimates from which you can derive the cash flow item. Your first step is to identify and work with the best sources for forecast data. Note that the same person may not be able to provide forecast data for all time horizons covered by your various forecasts.

Examples of sources categorized by type of data element and source are shown in Exhibit 7.4. By looking at your data items from these different perspectives, you should get a better feel for the ones that are difficult to forecast and which ones you are pretty sure of. You may find that one of the perspectives offers more confidence than the others. It will depend on your case—that's what makes forecasting so difficult and challenging. The items shown in the exhibit are not all-inclusive. You should adapt this list of sources to your situation.

Exhibit 7.4 Possible Sources for Forecasting Information

By Type of Data Element

Receipts—examples include:

Lockbox collections	Local office collections
Subs loans to parent	Corporate tax refunds
LT financing proceeds	ST debt proceeds
ST investments maturing	Export collections

Disbursements

Local payables	Payroll funding
Insurance payments	Consolidated tax payments
Corporate payables	FX purchases
Corporate dividends	ST debt repayments
New ST investments	

By Source (i.e., staff vs. operating unit)

From corporate staff

Tax payments	Insurance payments
Pension fund payments	FX transactions
Payroll	ST investmt/debt transactions
Interest payments	Stock dividend payments

From operating units

Lockbox collections	Customer remittances
Local deposits	Export collections
Trade payable disbursements	Local payrolls

By Degree of Certainty or Predictability

Highly predictable

Payroll	Taxes
Dividends	Pension fund payments
ST investment maturities	Loan repayments

Somewhat predictable

Lockbox collections	LT financing
Export collections	Trade payable disbursements
Customer remittances	Foreign sub dividends

Highly unpredictable

FX transactions	Acquisitions
Asset sales (e.g., inventory)	Foreign investments
LT investments	Divestitures

You are most likely to have a list of sources that has entries from all three of the categories shown above. Remember, your sources are likely to change over time.

Translating estimates

What do you do if your daily forecast seems impossible to correct? The most obvious reason is that your sources are not reliable. It could be that they are being asked to predict something that they do not know—i.e., they are being asked to predict when deposits will clear, when all they know is when the deposits are made.

For instance, your credit manager may be able to estimate when customers will mail in their payments, but you are interested in when those payments will actually be deposited and be available as good funds. Similarly, your payables manager may only be able to tell you when checks are issued and mailed to vendors when what you want to know is when the checks will clear back against your account. In cases like these, you will have to determine when the actual cash flows are likely to occur and show those dates on your rolling daily cash forecast. This makes it more difficult to forecast accurately, but over time you should be able to develop standard timing to use in adjusting the estimated flows supplied by your sources. You should analyze each element in your daily forecast to determine whether there is a better, more reliable way to estimate cash flows.

The solution is to work with what the sources know and add to that what you should know. For instance, if your source knows when a customer is likely to pay, you can add time to that date to estimate when the funds will be available to your company. Likewise, if your source knows when checks are being distributed, you should be able to add on additional time, based on historical patterns, to estimate when the checks will clear.

Remember, once you receive cash projections from your data sources, the forecast becomes *yours*. This means that you cannot shift the blame back to the source. You can determine whether your sources are providing good estimates or not by regularly measuring variances between the estimates and the actual cash flows. Tracking historical cash flows and estimates should give you a good picture of how well your sources have estimated their cash flows.

Accuracy and Reliability

A forecast has to be accurate, but—and this is a key point to consider—it does not have to be *too* accurate. The level of accuracy in a forecast should be dictated by its use and the length of its forecasting horizon. For instance, a short-term forecast for the next 5-10 days has to be very accurate (it probably requires the highest degree of accuracy), because most errors here cannot be reversed in time to eliminate their impact. On the other hand, a monthly forecast for the next year or a yearly forecast for the next five years, does not require this same level of accuracy. This may make it easier for data providers to overcome fears of not knowing exactly what is going to happen.

Reliability is different from accuracy but is still an important factor in developing good forecasts. What I means by *reliable* is consistency—i.e., a source is reliable if the information provided is consistent over time. This means that if sources consistently underestimate disbursements, you can recognize this and adjust the forecast accordingly. If sources are inconsistent, you may have problems in how to treat their estimates because you cannot depend (or rely) on them to be consistently high or low. You need to identify the inconsistent sources first, so you can work with them to obtain consistent (and accurate) estimates.

A good forecast should be organized so that you can obtain the actual data from other sources as well as your regular providers of data. You should consider using your bank as a source for actual data to compare with the estimates shown on the forecast. You may find the data you need from the daily account detail or balance reports, the monthly account analysis statements, or the regular bank account statements. You may have to get the information from your bank because you have translated a source's input.

⇒Get Started!

Analyze Your Current System

Start by evaluating your current forecasting capabilities. You can use the following checklist as a guide. Your answers to these questions will help create the proper perspective in evaluating your forecasting capabilities and what must be done to improve the current situation.

Checklist: Determining Present Capabilities

1. What are the major uses for the current system?
    - Short-range uses?
    - Longer-term uses?

2. How well has the current system performed?
    - Judge by major errors, surprises, etc.
    - Poll major users about this. Do they use something else to make decisions?
    - Has one aspect of the forecasting worked better than others? If so, can the system be rebuilt or improved by building from this area?

3. How difficult is the current system to use?
    - How long does it take to produce current system reports?
    - How many people are involved in preparing the forecast(s)?
    - Are some data items harder to pull together than others? What do the providers of information suggest?

---

4. How automated is the forecasting system?
   - Is data collection automated, semi-automated, or manual?
   - Are the final forecasts entered into computer form, e.g., on to a spreadsheet program? Is this program standard throughout the company (so its format can be used to collect data)?
   - How many data items are forecast?
   - By each forecasting source?
   - For the forecast overall?
5. What level of detail is required?
   - Are you asking sources to predict beyond their capabilities or responsibilities?
   - How often is the level reviewed?
6. How accurate is the current system?
   - Have levels of accuracy been established? How is accuracy measured?
   - Is there a different expectation by type of forecast?
   - How reliable have the forecasts been?
   - Has reliability been improving or deteriorating?
7. Have the sources of forecasting data been actively involved in the overall forecasting process?
   - If not, how can they be brought into it?
   - If so, has the feedback been constructive and timely?
8. What major errors have occurred in the recent past (e.g., past six months)?
   - What were they caused by?
   - What steps were taken to avoid future recurrences?
   - Potential automated links

8

Global Cash Positions

Today's global economy means it is likely businesses have trading partners in other countries. Interaction with these customers directly or indirectly through local subsidiaries in foreign countries affects the cash position like other cash flows. If you receive or make international funds transfers regularly, you should incorporate this into your daily cash position management.

The main problem with foreign cash flows is when you are notified of the receipt of the funds—i.e., because of time zone differences, foreign funds transfers may come in during your business day. This means that you will have to set up same-day information reporting for international transfers.

Companies that operate globally may buy and sell foreign currencies, finance foreign trade through letters of credit, and handle cross-border payments and receipts. All these activities can affect your cash position when they occur, so the groups who handle them must be included as part of your overall cash management system and their activities must be captured within your bank information reporting network.

Differences in overseas banking systems and cash management practices can affect the movements of funds into or out of a country or place other restrictions on doing business within a country's borders. Large multinational banks can help you with cross-border funds movements. You should use one of them if you expect funds transfers to or from many foreign sources. If your major bank happens to have extensive foreign branches, you can easily incorporate international funds movements into your daily cash position management.

Even smaller regional banks have the capabilities to act as portals for companies to domestic and global payment systems. Companies can now make payments electronically anywhere in the world through their desktop computers.

Managing a Foreign Sub's Cash Position

In most cases you will not be able to actively manage the cash position of a foreign subsidiary on a real-time basis because of time zone differences and, in some cases, the lack of critical balance and transaction data. If you have a small operation that is essentially a branch that needs its expenses handled, you may be able to do that from your office. It all depends on the location. If your overseas office is in a major city, such as London or Hong Kong, you should be able to manage its expenses from the U.S.

Handling the time zone differences can be difficult, depending on your location and the locations of your foreign subs. For instance, you may have a small window of opportunity to manage a European sub's position, but you would not be able to do so for an Asian sub because of time zone differences. In most cases, your best bet is to have the positions actually handled in-country by a financial manager at your foreign sub or by a regional treasury group in a major financial center, such as London. You can monitor the results by receiving daily reports that show the day's activity and closing positions.

If you wish to manage your foreign subs' cash positions centrally, there is another problem besides time zone differences that you must deal with—information services from local banks. In many banking systems, balances are not regularly reported and are subject to change retroactively through a process called value dating. The availability of deposits in these countries is deferred to future business dates, a process which is analogous to the deferred availability that U.S. banks assess on check deposits.

The problem comes with disbursements, which can be back valued by the bank, a process that is not found in the U.S. banking system. (Note that U.S. banks do back value by processing "as of" adjustments when resolving error, such as misdirected funds transfer.) Thus, your balance today could change tomorrow, which might mean that if you reduce today's balances too much, you could be in an overdraft position for today's balance.

Overdrafts in foreign banking systems are handled by having facilities in place to treat them as short-term loans. Foreign overdraft systems treat overdrafts more automatically than the U.S. banking system does.

The first step, then, in considering foreign cash positions is to determine how susceptible the balances are to back value dating. If this is the case, you will need to compute the average back value and use it as a target balance to avoid bank overdraft charges. Because of the ease of handling overdrafts, many cash managers have not actively tried to manage their daily cash position. Of course, this does not mean that you cannot try to manage it more actively.

With the growth of more advanced cross-border banking services through key markets, such as across Europe where the euro is the common currency, bank information systems are able to report balances regularly. Companies should be pushing to eliminate value dating type compensation practices and pushing for more fee-based compensation to be able to manage their cash position more closely. This means you should expect to be able to manage your European cash position across all the countries you have operations in once the banking systems allow you to move funds easily throughout the common euro area.

International Cash Management

When dealing globally, there are two perspectives that you need to keep in mind—one for the individual country and one for the global or cross-border viewpoint. To handle the in-country perspective, you will need to understand how the banking system works, what services banks offer, and how treasury is (or can be) practiced in the country. In the past, learning about each country was difficult, but with more recent developments, such as the adoption of the euro across most of Europe and the growing focus on treasury practices by banks as well as trade groups, it is becoming easier to establish effective treasury practices in your foreign subs.

The second perspective is global. In this case there are bank-provided and internally provided services that many large multinational companies have used for years. They are not really targeted for smaller companies. The major techniques used include:

Pooling

Intra-company offsets result in interest given or charged on net amount within a given country. This is usually done for a single currency within a single country where you have a large number of subsidiaries, although European banks do offer cross-border and multi-currency pooling. Pooling helps you manage your cash position by offsetting all of your accounts, so you can see your position with the bank easily and decide whether to invest the excess funds or borrow to offset deficits. Obviously, pooling is more advantageous when you can consolidate your banking needs with a single bank.

Leading and Lagging

This technique involves moving funds from cash-rich subs to cash-poor ones, rather than seek outside financing. As was the case with pooling, you need a fairly large number of locations to consider using this technique. To do this, you need to be able to track cash positions and cash flow forecasts at your foreign subs. This technique can help you in managing cash positions, but it has to be effected by changing credit terms and payment timings. Even if you can handle these requirements, you may still face a major difficulty in getting accurate information on the positions and projected cash flows from your foreign banks and subs. Many companies find it easier to negotiate a short-term borrowing facility that covers all your foreign locations.

Netting

Large multinational companies with many foreign subs that have heavy volumes of business with each other and with the parent company and domestic operating units establish netting systems to cut down on duplicated cash flows. This helps manage your cash positions because you only have to deal with the net difference between trading locations. This reduces the amount of cash needed by each sub. Netting can be bilateral—between two countries (or one country with the parent)—or multilateral—among all participating units. The netting transactions typically occur monthly when only the net amounts are transferred. A netting center, which is usually part of the treasury group and can be located at the parent office or at an overseas location, handles the transactions and information reporting. With this system, netting participants receive advanced notice of how much they will receive or have to pay in sufficient time to determine the effect on their cash positions. Netting systems are primarily used for transactions within the same corporation, not with outside parties.

Reinvoicing [Center]

A reinvoicing center works similarly to a netting center, except it is not restricted to intra-corporate transactions. It is also intended for very large multinational corporations. The center takes title to goods being shipped and rebills (or reinvoices) the goods for sale to the trading party. This technique will not be useful unless you have a substantial amount of international business. If you do, it can help your cash position management on cross-border shipments by centralizing foreign exchange needs as well as providing cash flow forecasts on cross-border activities.

Foreign Exchange

Foreign exchange (FX) transactions add another set of cash flows that affect your cash position. Companies of all sizes can have FX transactions, but larger companies tend to be the heaviest users of these services. FX transactions are not difficult to complete, but you need to learn how the mechanics of FX trading are handled in order to manage these transactions as part of your cash position. Your banks should be willing to help you learn the steps you must go through in making FX transactions. You need this familiarity to be able to gauge the impact of FX trades on your cash position.

Foreign exchange fundamentals

FX rates for foreign currencies (with respect to the U.S. dollar) are usually expressed in terms of the amount of foreign currency per dollar. For instance, if Japanese yen are said to be "trading at 150," this means that the exchange rate is 150 yen (¥) per dollar. The major exception to this rule is the British pound sterling (£). Rates for the pound-dollar exchange are quoted as dollars per pound.

FX rates are published in most financial newspapers or financial sections of newspapers daily. The official rates set by the U.S. central bank, the Federal Reserve, are posted daily on the Federal Reserve's Web site.

Dealing with a customer or vendor in another country may require dealing in a foreign currency. Companies enter the FX markets via banks that sell foreign currency or purchase it, usually at rates that change continually (i.e., floating rates). FX trades (sales or purchases) are settled at an agreed-upon future date and payment is made electronically, usually through transactions involving the CHIPS and S.W.I.F.T. payment systems.

There are two types of FX markets — spot and forward. The *spot market* is for "immediate" purchase or sale between two currencies. Spot transactions made by U.S. companies are settled in one or two business days, depending on the country (e.g., Canada settles in one day; European currencies in two). There is a program currently available and growing in volume that settles FX contracts faster than these one- or two-day time periods for spot transactions. Your bank may offer you the possibility of closing spot contracts sooner for an additional fee.

In a forward FX transaction, called a *forward contract*, a company and its bank agree on the purchase or sale of one currency for another at a future date for a negotiated rate. A forward, by definition, has to be for two or three (depending on the currency) days or more in the future. Forward exchange rates are based on the spot rate and the interest rates between the countries whose currencies are involved. Forward rates are available for most major currencies for practically any length of time, although the market is largely up to one year. The possible availability of far-out dates will depend on the currencies involved.

When both parties agree to the FX transaction, they give settlement instructions that specify where to transfer the funds to complete the trade. In order to enter into forward contracts with a bank, customers are generally required to have a line of credit in place specifically for this purpose.

Effect on cash position

FX trades can impact your cash position quickly in cases of spot contracts that were unplanned, although you may have one or two business days' notice before the funds are due to be paid out. If you are making a trade with your bank, you and the banker will agree upon the exchange rate and verify the amounts of currency involved.

You settle FX contracts by transferring funds electronically, based on instructions you and the bank agree on at the time of the trade. (For forward contracts, the instructions can be finalized at a later date, if necessary.) You usually settle FX trades by using the CHIPS (Clearing House Interbank Payment System) for U.S. dollar transfers and SWIFT (Society for Worldwide Interbank Financial Telecommunication) for foreign currencies. If you are dealing with one of the large, multinational banks, the transfers may be handled through the bank's own network, but usually CHIPS and SWIFT are used.

Once you complete a spot or forward trade, the data should be entered into your rolling maturity schedule (described earlier). This will help you in preparing for future cash positions.

Foreign currency accounts

Companies engaged in two-way trade (both buying from and selling to the same country) or that have foreign subsidiaries often want to maintain foreign currency demand deposit accounts and short-term, interest-bearing deposits denominated in a foreign currency. This is done to avoid the cost of converting the currency to U.S. dollars and then back again. These accounts may also be part of a foreign exchange risk management program built around naturally offsetting foreign currency-denominated assets and liabilities on the company's balance sheet.

Some banks offer foreign currency *call accounts* that reside in the U.S. These are accounts denominated in a foreign currency that are maintained on the books of the U.S. bank for its customers. Customers can deposit payments to these accounts denominated in the respective foreign currency, maintain the balances,

111

and remit funds from these accounts in the form of wires or (paper) drafts. Balance reporting on and funds transfer initiation from these accounts can be processed through the bank's information reporting system. Companies may also request that their bank provide them with credit facilities denominated in the foreign currency to support liquidity management needs in these currencies.

Companies considering establishing offshore operations also will need to consider opening operating accounts in the country of the subsidiary. Depending on the degree of treasury management centralization, the U.S. treasury manager may want to receive account balance reporting to monitor the local operating accounts. This can be accomplished between banks through the transmission of SWIFT messages from the foreign bank to the company's U.S. bank. Some banks have the ability to incorporate this information in their information reporting systems.

Foreign currency accounts may help in managing your cash position by supplying the currencies you need without having to engage in a trade. Their outstanding balances should be monitored and managed against target balance levels.

Making cross-border payments

Companies of all sizes may have to make cross-border funds transfers. Just like settling FX transactions, when making other international (cross-border) funds transfers electronically, you use the SWIFT network, an inter-bank system, or the CHIPS system. For companies with frequent international payments, banks provide international wire transfer services that are similar to those used for domestic wire transfers, except that the bank locations are overseas. Many of these services can be set up through a bank's information reporting system for recurring transactions. For special transactions or low-value transactions, companies may call their banks by phone to make the transfer. In any case, these transfers will affect your cash position just like any other transfer.

For one-time, small payments in a foreign currency, banks and a few non-bank firms offer a paper-based draft service. The amount of foreign currency is requested, and the equivalent in U.S. dollars is paid to the draft provider. The draft is mailed or delivered to the company for final use. The company then mails the draft to the party owed the funds. Fees for this service are either explicitly stated or are reflected in the conversion rate. These transactions should not be substantial, so they should have minimal impact on your cash position. You use this service for transactions that are too small for regular FX trades. Most banks offering this service will supply you with guidelines for using the service.

For incoming transfers in U.S. dollars, the amounts and details will be shown on reports from the bank's information reporting system. Amounts in a foreign currency may be shown, or they may be automatically routed to the bank's FX area for conversion to U.S. dollars, which then would be shown on the report. This automatic conversion must be arranged between the company and its bank beforehand. You should see these transactions on your daily bank information reports.

9

Getting Started

Now it's time to take the plunge and begin managing your cash position. If you will need to make changes, you'll have to make them as you go, since cash position management isn't something you can set aside for awhile until you have made the required changes.

To gain the most from your efforts you should assign priorities to the changes you'll need to make. For instance, if your sources for cash flow information have not been effective, you may need to tackle this first. You cannot protect your organization's cash resources very well if you don't know much about the cash flows. You can try to react to the cash flow information as you receive, but trust me, this gets to be onerous in no time.

Your set of priorities may differ from another person's because of the differences in cash flow size, cash flow timing, effectiveness of current information reporting sources, and lines of business. Working with the priorities, it makes sense to tackle the highest-priority items first, unless making a change will take a very long time—e.g., months or longer.

Putting the Pieces Together

There are several components of cash position management that you will need in your implementation plan. None of these items should be impossible to set up. Done correctly, they comprise an effective system for managing your position:

Cash position worksheet

You will need a worksheet for your daily cash position management. This can be a simpler spreadsheet model that records daily cash inflows and outflows *from your vantage point*. These are the flows that you must manage. Much of the data from a daily worksheet may carry over to the next day's worksheet, and so on. You may wish to have several days or the next week (five business days) in front of you at all times, so you'll need to accommodate this on your daily worksheet.

If you plan to use a spreadsheet model, you should use the workbook function that spreadsheet programs offer to keep your day-today activities well organized and to permit easy lookups for historical cash flow information.

For very large corporations, more than a simple spreadsheet model may be required, depending on how complex the corporation's cash flows are and how many major banks it maintains. If both the number of cash flows and the number of banks are lengthy, a more sophisticated system—e.g., a treasury work station—will typically be required.

Information Reporting Service

You will need effective information reporting services that include all your major banks. The availability of this data is a critical element in the daily cash position management cycle. If this is inefficient or not organized effectively, managing the overall position becomes more difficult. In cases like this, you have to be able to fix your system while operating it at the same time. If you can streamline your system by reducing the number of banks involved in your network, it may make it mush easier to manage your cash position.

For smaller organizations, simple balance reports and detailed transaction summaries may be sufficient. Remember, you only need information to manage the position. Don't try to pack in as much information as you can get because you may obscure the really time-critical information.

For larger corporations, you may have the need to tap numerous sources of information, so your system will be more complex than a smaller company's system.

Funds transfer services

You will need to be able to transfer funds to and from your major banks. Having these services readily available is one of the key determinants in how mobilized your funds can be. Here again size makes a difference. Smaller organizations will probably not need much funds transfer capability, while larger ones will depend on having effective transfer services.

Potential Problems and Solutions

What could go wrong? The easy answer is, "Anything." The hard answer is, "Everything." Reality on any given day probably lies between these two extremes.

In Exhibit 9.1, I discuss what I think are the most common problems you will encounter in managing your cash position and offer my solution to the problems. I recognize that my solutions may not be the only possible ones. Also, note that the solutions to different problems may be the same.

Moving Ahead

With the piece described above you should be up and running smoothly in no time. You will find that managing your position is anything but routine. If you have established a sound support system that incorporates the best available sources of information and information technology into your daily system, you should be able to manage your position efficiently. However, your cash position can change, often with sudden speed, so you cannot coast—this is an ongoing concern at companies large and small. You should always have the attitude that you can keep doing it better.

Exhibit 9.1 Potential Problems and Solutions

Potential Problems	Potential Solutions
Information is not available from the bank. What do you do?	Extrapolate from your last report yesterday, using your short-term forecast for today's activity. Change the estimates when you get good data. – or – Refer back to your history (you did maintain it, didn't you?). Go with the average. – or – Call your banker. He or she may have access to the data that you do not have.
You download your report, but it doesn't have all the information you usually get. What do you do?	Call your banker. He or she may have access to the data that you do not have. – or – Go with your forecast and correct things later on in the day. – or – Look at your records for this day last month or last year to get a better idea on the magnitude of cash flows and whether you are likely to face a net cash inflow or outflow.
Several operating units and corporate staff departments have consistently been providing inaccurate short-term forecasts and do not seem to be getting better. What do you do?	Set up a meeting to discuss the situation, doing your "homework" first to be able to show how well the units have been doing. Bring along a report card if you keep one. – and – Consider bringing along some "heavy artillery," such as your boss or another senior financial executive.

Potential Problems	Potential Solutions
A last-minute (new) funding request "appears." How do you handle this?	First determine whether the surprise truly has to be handled today and cannot be put off for a day (use borrowing or Fedwire cutoffs as a possible excuse). If it must be handled today, determine if you have enough funds (e.g., as a target balance that you could temporarily draw down) or tap your "emergency" fund (i.e., a small deposit or bank line set aside for just this purpose).
You find out that bank transfers are being made by a "maverick" unit and you are possibly blocked by organizational barriers. How do you handle it?	First check with senior financial executives to see if the activity needs to be stopped immediately (e.g., it is in violation of a lending agreement or other legal agreement). If the activity is not ruled out, contact the unit or schedule a meeting with the unit to discuss why the unit wants to do something that you are fully capable of doing and are supposed to, as part of your job description. – or – Call on a senior financial executive to "negotiate" a halt to the process. Note that to do this you will have to show how it is hurting the company.
You receive a large international transfer from an overseas customer that shows up in your same-day report at 12:30. What is your reaction?	Check your same-day report to be sure the transfer has been received and that you can determine who sent it and whether you need to convert from a foreign currency. Once assured, treat it like any other cash receipt and use it as a source of cash. – or – Ask your bank (assuming it was one of your major banks who received the funds) to roll the money overnight, possibly in a Euro$ time deposit.

Potential Problems	Potential Solutions
It is taking you and your three colleagues 5-6 hours daily just to manage all the bank information. What can you do to relieve the situation?	Explore automated help, such as a treasury work station, assuming you have the budget for it. Ask for competitive bids by supplying prospective vendors with a request for proposal that contains your requirements. Ask for in-depth, in-site demonstrations from key vendors. – or – Consider a major review of your practices and procedures. You can try this internally or hire a consultant to do it for you.
You find out that several units are making payments before they provide the information to central treasury. What do you do?	Contact the unit or schedule a meeting with the unit to discuss why the unit wants to do something that you are fully capable of doing and are supposed to, as part of your job description. – or – Call on a senior financial executive to "negotiate" a halt to the process. Note that to do this you will have to show how it is hurting the company.
You "discover" that several units have hoarded sub-stantial amounts of cash in their local bank accounts, earning interest on the balances via a sweep account. The sweep interest rate is 2.00%. Your average short-term borrowing rate is 7.25%. What do you want to do?	Call on a senior financial executive to "negotiate" a halt on the process. Note that to do this you will have to show how it is hurting the company, which should be fairly easy to do (2% gain vs. 7% opportunity cost).

Potential Problems	Potential Solutions
Your supervisor keeps track of the company's cash, but on its books, not what's in the bank. Do you want to do anything about this?	First, determine what your supervisor is doing with the cash number. If it is not going to have any effect on your job or how the cash position is managed, you may want to do nothing.
	Schedule a session with your supervisor and possibly with your banker to discuss the differences between the company's books and the values that should be used as part of managing cash and the cash position.
You have worked to set target balances at your three major banks, but you find that the targets are too low to be achieved. What can you do?	The obvious answer is raise the target, but you may want to check the history to determine if there is a seasonal effect .
	– or –
	Analyze the bank balances and the bank services to determine whether you can make a change that will free up balances sooner. For instance, you may try wiring funds out instead of using the ACH.
	If the balances are so high that they provide more than enough compensation for the cash management services you use, you may wish to switch from a target balance and earn interest on the balances by using a sweep service.
You want to determine how far out you can schedule your investments or borrowings. What do you need to make the decision?	You will need a good, reliable forecast.
	You will also need a history of your cash flows for the near-term future to help identify possible swings in cash balances.
	You will need a maturity schedule.
	All of these items can be entered and tracked on a spreadsheet model.

Potential Problems	Potential Solutions
You receive a call from your largest operating unit with an urgent request to make a substantial wire transfer (domestic) after you've finished all your work and established your positions. How do you handle this?	First determine whether the surprise truly has to be handled today and cannot be put off for a day (use borrowing or Fedwire cutoffs as a possible excuse). If it does, determine if you have enough funds (e.g., as a target balance that you could temporarily draw down) or tap your "emergency" fund (i.e., a small deposit or bank line set aside for just this purpose). If this emergency fund is not sufficient, throw yourself at the mercy of your banker.

Appendix A

Short-Term Investing

Overview

Proper management of a company's short-term investments requires a formal company policy with guidelines that clearly state the purpose of the portfolio and describe eligible investment securities. The degree of risk and return a company can tolerate will determine, to a large extent, which short-term securities it chooses and the strategy it will follow in managing its short-term investment portfolio.

It is tempting to look for the highest return on these funds, but this means taking on excess risk. As a result, companies with relatively small amounts of short-term investments usually follow conservative investing practices, trading off higher rates (and risks) for safety and liquidity.

Short-Term Investment Strategies

One of the simplest strategies is a passive one, where a company follows predetermined rules. The strategy may consist of buying securities and holding them until they mature. At maturity, the outstanding investment balance is reduced by the amount of funds needed elsewhere or increased by further excesses. This new excess is "rolled over" into a new issue of the same or comparable security for another set time period or to a different maturity. This "buy and hold" approach is done routinely (e.g., daily as necessary) and is easy to administer and measure.

A second passive strategy uses *repurchase agreements*. A repurchase agreement (repo) involves several linked steps. First, the securities dealer sells the securities to the investor. At the same time, the dealer enters into an agreement to buy back (or *repurchase*) the securities at a future time for a future amount that includes the interest on the investment. At the time of the investment, the dealer transfers title of the securities purchased to the investor. The securities may be held by an independent third party—often the company's bank—in safekeeping until the maturity date. On maturity, the custody-holder, on behalf of the investor, returns the securities to the dealer, and the company receives its funds back with interest (as per their agreement). Many firms use repos for very short-term investments, rolling over their investments nightly.

Another approach is to combine a passive strategy with a more active one, such as matching. This entails identifying specific cash outflows, such as payroll taxes or long-term debt repayments, and purchasing a short-term investment to mature on the day the funds are needed. Matching securities can be bought and held (by the company's custody and safekeeping bank) until the maturity date, when they will provide the cash flow that is required. If the date of the cash need cannot be identified precisely beforehand, the company can time the investment to mature early and use repos that can be rolled over each night until the funds are required. Buying securities with longer maturities usually means better (higher) returns.

Banks offer custody services that keep track of a company's short-term portfolio. Some banks can also produce inventory and maturity reports on the portfolio through their information reporting system.

Types of Short-Term Investments

There are many types of short-term investment instruments. Companies with larger amounts of funds (e.g., more than $5 million to $10 million on average) often purchase money market securities directly from broker-dealers. These instruments differ by their source (e.g., the federal government, corporations, and banks) and degree of safety. Safety is usually measured by low risk and high liquidity, i.e., the ability of a security to be converted to cash on demand. Rates vary by the degree of risk associated with a security and its time to maturity. (See table.)

U.S. Treasury bills (t-bills) are considered the safest and most liquid short-term investment security because they are backed by the full faith and credit of the United States government. T-bills have never suffered a default. They also have a substantial secondary (resale) market, which means that they can be sold at any time for the current market value. This makes them a popular and virtually risk-free investment. Their low risk means that t-bills offer the lowest returns. T-bills are sold on a discounted basis. That is, the investor pays the face value of the bills less the discount and receives back the face value at maturity.

U.S. federal government agencies, such as the Federal Home Loan Board, issue securities that are almost as safe as t-bills and are also very popular. In addition, rates on federal agencies' securities are somewhat higher than t-bill rates. Agency securities are sold on an interest-bearing (i.e., not discount) basis, which means that the investor receives back principal and interest on maturity. There is also a good secondary market for these securities.

Short-term investments are not limited to government securities. For example, bank certificates of deposit (CDs) are a form of time deposit and are usually sold for a fixed time and a fixed rate on an interest-bearing basis.

Another security that can be used as part of a short-term portfolio is commercial paper (CP). Corporations, financial companies, and bank holding companies issue commercial paper in the form of unsecured, short-term notes with maturities up to 270 days, with heavy concentration on 30-day periods. Companies with short-term portfolios also may invest in banker's acceptances (BAs), which are money market securities created by banks with underlying corporate trade transactions, usually international in nature. Both CP and BAs are sold on a discounted basis, like t-bills.

Exhibit A.1 Short-term Investment Instruments

Instrument	Maturity Range	Discount or Interest	Notes/Comments
U.S. Treasury Bills	13, 26, 52 wks.	Discount	Obligations of U.S. Treasury; active secondary market; highest safety
Federal Agencies	5 days-20 yrs.	Interest (mostly)	Considered default free; slightly less liquid than t-bills; active secondary market
Banker's Acceptances	30-270 days	Discount	Corporate *Time Deposits*; accepted by banks; triple protection; active secondary market
Domestic CDs	14-365 days	Interest	$100,000 min. investment; yield based on issuer's credit—more for Yankee CDs; fixed or variable; active secondary market
Bank Notes	14-365 days	Interest	Variation on CDs; no reserve requirements; do not have to be constantly rolled over (like CDs); not deposits; no FDIC coverage
Eurodollar Deposits	1-180 days	Interest	Time deposits or CDs; some liquidity risk
US Commercial Paper (CP)	1-270 days	Discount (typically)	Usually a 30-day market; unsecured corporate noes; ratings and back-up liquidity required; active support by mutual funds
Euro-CP	1-365 days	Discount (typically)	Rated securities; small market
Repurchase Agreements	1 day+	Discount	Sale of security with agreement to repurchase; typically very short maturities—overnight to one week or so; typically overcollateralized
Mutual Funds and Money Market Funds	1 day+	Interest	Money market funds very safe source, used by smaller firms; as safe as underlying securities; can be linked to sweep services
Sweep Accounts	1 day+	Depends on the security	Essentially overnight, but can be moved into smaller denominated instruments such as mutual funds (MMMFs) or into larger ones such as Euro TDs, T-bills, or money market securities
Other Variable Rate instruments	1, 7 days	Interest	Variable Rate Demand Notes (VRDNs) issued in various maturities; denominations start at $100,000; often tax exempt

126

These securities trade actively and have a moderate secondary market, but they are not considered as safe or liquid as the U.S. t-bills and agencies. They also have more credit or default risk than t-bills and agencies and offer higher rates of return. Issuers obtain ratings on their short-term debt, usually from one or both of the two major rating agencies—Standard & Poor's and Moody's.

Sweep services

Smaller companies and companies with investable funds less than $5 million may be better served by money market mutual funds and bank sweep services that provide automatic investments and high liquidity. Sweeps work by transferring, or *sweeping*, all funds in excess of a minimum balance (predetermined by the bank and the company) into an investment account at the end of the business day and returning the invested funds plus interest to the company's account, usually on the next business day or as needed. They have become one of the most popular services that companies use because they can be arranged to work automatically. For many companies they are the simplest and easiest way to invest short-term funds.

Sweeps are not restricted to overnight arrangements. Sweep services can be set up to move funds over a set (imprest or pegged) level into an investment account, such as a money market mutual fund, or into a prearranged short-term investment portfolio.

All sweeps are not simply investment arrangements. Some are designed to help a company manage its cash position. With a variation called a *credit sweep account*, the bank will automatically draw on a company's line of credit to bring a negative account balance up to zero, thus covering any potential overdrafts. When the account balance is positive, the bank will automatically pay down the line of credit and then sweep any excess into a prearranged investment.

127

Appendix B

Financing Cash Needs

Types of Short-Term Borrowing

A line of credit allows a company to borrow up to the amount of the line for a specified time, usually a year. As long as a company has a satisfactory repayment history and has had no significant (bad) occurrences, such as a major operating loss or financial crisis, its line of credit should be available when needed and renewable yearly.

The "regular" line of credit that most companies arrange is called a *committed line of credit* because the bank "commits" that the line (maximum amount) is available. A committed line of credit is usually unsecured by any company assets or guarantees, and it can be prepaid without any penalties.

Pricing for a committed line of credit includes interest on the amount borrowed, usually set as a fraction over a money market rate, such as the London Interbank Offered Rate (LIBOR), or at the bank's prime rate. Companies with weaker credit standing can expect to pay more in interest than firms with good credit standing. The other major cost of a line of credit is compensation to the bank for the line. This is typically in the form of a commitment fee. Commitment fees are usually paid quarterly and generally are set at a fraction of one percent of the full line or just the amount that is unused.

Banks also offer *uncommitted lines of credit* that can function like regular lines. However, as the name suggests, these lines are not always available. Uncommitted lines, which do not require the explicit compensation of regular lines, can be used for one-time or infrequent borrowing. They also can be set up to cover situations where the bank wants to place a limit on financial transactions other than lines, such as foreign exchange or daylight overdrafts. In essence, it is appropriate to think of uncommitted lines as a mechanism to complete a financial transaction between a bank and its corporate customer.

Larger firms that use the money markets for short-term borrowings issue *commercial paper* (CP) through a dealer. The CP market is a very large one, and most companies have no trouble in satisfying their short-term cash needs by issuing CP. CP can be issued for any maturity, but the most common are 30, 60, 90, and 180 days. The maximum maturity is 270 days, since this represents the longest maturity that an instrument can have without having to be registered with the Securities and Exchange Commission.

Because CP is sold at a discount, the issuer (the borrower) receives less than the face amount issued. The amount received is the face amount less the interest. Upon maturity, the borrower pays back the face amount. For example, if a company issues $10 million in commercial paper for 30 days at 6%, it will receive $9,950,000 ($10 million less the interest: $10 million time 6 percent times 30/360). The interest is calculated on a 360-day "year" for money market securities.

A revolving credit agreement is used primarily by mid-sized and larger corporations. It includes a written legal agreement and is often arranged with a group of banks (a syndicate). The pricing is similar to a committed line, except that a revolving credit agreement also has legal fees and additional fees for providing the credit (facility fees). Revolving credit agreements are often arranged for more than year and may contain a long-term borrowing option that allows the borrower to convert the outstanding short-term borrowings to a long-term form of borrowing, such as a 5-7 year term loan.

Certain borrowers, such as companies that are undergoing rapid growth or have seen their credit position weakened significantly, may be required by a bank lender to provide collateral to securitize the lending arrangement. Collateral may be a pledge of the company's accounts receivable (subject to the bank's acceptance) or another asset, such as inventory or possibly a long-term asset, such as a plant or office building. This type of arrangement is also known as *asset-based financing* (ABF) and is often tailored to the specific characteristics of the business assets. The pledged assets create a borrowing base that fluctuates with growth and seasonality and may be accessed at any time or paid down without penalty.

Short-Term Debt Strategies

Three basic aspects of a sound borrowing policy are diversity, flexibility, and availability.

Diversity means having adequate alternative forms, e.g., types of bank lines, avoiding too much reliance on one type or lowest rate, and is especially important in times of credit limitations. Often, borrowers will trade off short-term rate advantages to assure diversity.

A strategy should also have flexibility in maturities to be able to match cash needs or to synchronize cash outflows with expected cash inflows. Borrowing facilities should also be easy to use. There should also be a low minimum size, so that a borrower can move freely from one form to another. Strategies should also have flexibility in the borrowing rate, with more than one option, such as prime, money market, or LIBOR.

Availability means using types of facilities that are based on strong primary and secondary markets, such as commercial paper. This also means that borrowers should try to stay with standard forms of borrowing instruments and avoid getting locked into a specialized form created only for them, such as an exotic derivative, which then "traps" the borrower.

Often, the best strategy is to approach short-term borrowing as if you were managing a short-term debt "portfolio." This should tie your short-term strategy and activities into the firm's overall liquidity strategy. It will encourage maintaining a cost-effective form of borrowing that will usually be the lowest rate (but not necessarily—sometimes you borrow at a higher rate to keep sources open or to save cheaper sources for longer terms). It also means maintaining a mix of instruments to provide diversity and interest rate protection and optimal maturities that can be spread out efficiently.

Short-term borrowing can be passive, with minimal activity, probably one source or type, little if any planning. Borrowers fall into a roll-over "habit" in which loans are continually rolled over for the same period of time with little if any attention paid to the rate. This is a "take what you can get" approach and often translates into higher rates.

Effective short-term borrowing should be managed more actively. This is a more flexible strategy and requires planning, reliable forecasts, and active negotiations. It also may include a matching approach, where known or expected future cash flows are matched with short-term borrowing timed to mature on the expected date of the cash receipt.

Appendix C

Reconciliation and Positive Pay Services

Many companies today have in-house reconcilement systems as part of a broader enterprise resource planning (ERP) system and do not need full reconciliation from their banks. With *partial reconciliation*, companies receive lists of checks that cleared in check number sequence. This may be a simple printed report or an electronic file. The information is then entered into the in-house reconcilement system for final resolution of account balances.

Full reconciliation essentially balances the company's checking account monthly. The company sends its check issued file to the bank. The bank uses this file to reconcile the account, sending the company back the account balance, a list of items paid, and items still outstanding. Upon request, many of these systems can also provide a summary of check clearing times, which can be useful in cash forecasting.

Positive pay was developed to provide companies with a safeguard against check fraud. It works like a same-day reconcilement service. Companies using the service transmit files of checks issued to the bank whenever disbursements are made. The bank uses the accumulated check-issued files to verify each check it receives to be cleared against the company's account by comparing key data—e.g., check number and check amount. Some banks also check payee name, adding further protection. If the key data items match, the check is paid. If they do not match, the check is referred to the company for a pay/no-pay decision. This usually takes place one day after check clearing, and the company has a limited time to respond to the bank (times differ among banks). The company and bank prearrange a "default" action (e.g., pay or reject) that the bank uses if the company fails to respond by the deadline. Positive pay can be set up for any disbursement account and has proven to be a valuable service.

For companies that prefer to do all check reconcilement internally, banks offer a *reverse positive pay* arrangement. Reverse positive pay works like the regular positive pay service except that the bank transmits to the company a file of the checks it has received for payment, and the company does the checking. The company then sends an updated file back to the bank with the desired actions (e.g., pay, refuse, etc.) indicated.

Appendix D

Guidelines for Using Technology

How can you tell if a service based on a new technology is right for you? The following short checklist will help you evaluate a new technology:

What can technology do for you?

In looking at any technology, the first thing to learn is what the technology can do for you. This is important because you will not be able to successfully integrate a new technology without some overall objective. Typical goals are faster processing, better system integration, enhanced information, or lower costs.

How difficult is it to learn? Who handles training?

New technologies that are not upgrades or improvements but are truly new to your organization may take time to master. You should, through your preliminary research, determine how much time you or others in your organization will have to devote to understand the new technology. For more complex software or systems, a training specialist who understands the new technology may be a sound investment. Many software or systems providers offer additional training beyond installation for a fee.

What is the impact on your area and other areas?

You should also determine what the impact on your organization is likely to be. Although the new technology is probably targeted toward your area, you should consider its impact on other areas and include them in the implementation process, even if they only provide a review function. In assessing the impact, you should try to develop both the quantitative impact and the qualitative impact.

Who should be involved in decisions?

Identify specifically who will be involved in the decision-making and implementation activities. It makes sense to develop a list of people that will make up the implementation team. (See above.)

How long will it take to implement?

It is also necessary to develop a time plan for implementing a new technology. It should show when implementation activities will be light or heavy, and you can use this guideline as an aid to budgeting time and other resources.

What other implementation support will you need?

As you formulate your answers to these questions, you should be determining how much support you will need to implement the new technology. Then you can decide whether you will need any outside assistance or can manage everything with internal resources.

How much will it cost (and is it worth the cost)?

Finally, you should tackle the usual question for financial projects—estimating the costs of the new technology. The corollary is whether the cost is worth it. This is the final, pivotal question you need to answer. It is placed last on the list, but it could obviously be moved up in the list if desired.

Glossary of Treasury Management Terminology

account analysis statement – A bank report (separate from a bank statement) that provides the corporate customer with detailed account service data and charges. These statements are produced periodically (usually monthly) for each account with a summary for all accounts combined. The format for these statements differs somewhat from bank to bank despite the common standard developed by the AFP (see below) for banks to use in providing these reports to their customers.

account reconcilement – A bank service for corporate customers who agree to have the bank "balance" their checking account monthly. The bank provides the customer with a serial number listing of deposits and items paid or, by matching a list of items issued to the actual items paid, produces full reconcilement including outstanding items, balance by date, exceptions, and numerous optional reports.

addenda record – An ACH record type that carries the supplemental data needed to completely identify an account holder(s) or provide information concerning a payment to the Receiving Depository Financial Institution and the receiver.

advising bank – A bank selected to authenticate a letter of credit and pass it on to the beneficiary. An advising bank is typically a correspondent of the L/C issuing bank located in the country of the L/C beneficiary.

AFP - The Association for Financial Professionals

American National Standards Institute– A nonprofit organization engaged in the development of national standards. Membership comes from industry, trade associations, and the federal government. Special committees within ANSI deal with standards for bank cards and financial communication networks.

automated clearing house (ACH) – A regional distribution and settlement facility for interbank clearing of paperless entries for participating financial institutions.

automated investment service – See sweep arrangement

automated wholesale lockbox – A service in which the lockbox information is captured daily and transmitted electronically to the corporation.

available balance – The balance in an account that can be invested, disbursed or wired out. Available balance is defined as book balance less float. It is often referred to as collected balance.

availability – The number of days that elapse before funds deposited previously can be used, i.e., converted from ledger balances to collected or available balances, usually expressed in whole days, ranging from zero (0) to two (2) for most corporations.

average available balance – The sum of daily available balances in the account divided by the number of calendar days in the period. It usually appears on bank account analysis statements and bank statements. The balance for Friday is used for both Saturday and Sunday. Holidays use the balance figure from the previous business day.

BAI format – A standard [format] developed by the Bank Administration Institute that banks use to transmit data to their customers.

balance information reporting – See *information reporting system.*

banker's acceptance (BA) – Time drafts issued by firms, sold at a discount, that become negotiable instruments when they are accepted (endorsed) by the bank on which they are drawn. BA's arise in both foreign and domestic trade but are the financial responsibility of the accepting bank.

beneficiary – The seller of goods or services to whom a letter of credit is addressed and who is entitled to its benefits, i.e., payment.

bill of exchange – Another name for a draft

bill of lading – A document that establishes the terms of a contract between a shipper and a transportation company. It is prepared by the shipper using forms supplied by the carrier when freight is moved between specified points for a specified charge. A bill of lading serves as a document of title, a contract of carriage, and a receipt for goods.

book (or gross) balance – The bank ledger balance (or company general ledger balance) created when funds are deposited. It is the account balance on the bank's books before any reduction for float, uncollected funds or reserve requirements. It may also be used to refer to the amount of cash shown on a company's internal books (general ledger).

book entry – A system by which securities are bought and sold without a physical document or certificate.

cash concentration – The transfer of funds from diverse accounts at other banks or other bank accounts within the same bank into a central account at a company's concentration bank.

cash disbursement – The transfer of funds from a central account to diverse accounts to fund disbursements from those accounts.

cash item – Any item immediately convertible into cash such as an on-us check or currency.

cash letter (document) – A batch of checks that contains items drawn on the receiving bank as well as items drawn on many banks within or outside the region, accompanied by a letter detailing transit routings, amounts, and totals sent directly to a bank or processing center.

cash management account (CMA) – See *Master Account.*

certificate of deposit (CD) – A short-term security that represents a receipt for a time deposit at a commercial bank.

Check 21 – Federal legislation that established the rights of a payee or receiver of cash to convert paper checks to an electronic, digitized copy, which can be used to clear the check electronically. See also *IRDs* and *remote capture/deposit.*

check truncation – The process by which essential information contained on a paper check is captured electronically by the bank of first deposit, after which the electronic information—not the paper check—is sent through the clearing system. This may also be used to refer to a banking service where the customer does not receive cancelled checks with the regular statement.

CHIPS – The Clearing House Interbank Payment System, located in New York City, is a clearing and settlement facility for international U.S. dollar transactions for member banks that own and operate the system.

city and country points – Different classifications of banks or bank branch locations, depending on the location's geographic proximity to a Federal Reserve bank or branch, that the Federal Reserve uses to designate where checks are drawn and/or routed.

clearing – The process of collecting the cash represented by a paper check, by presenting the item at the drawee bank.

clearing house (local) – An organization established by banks in the same locality through which they exchange checks and other instruments and settle net balances daily.

collected balance – See *available balance.*

collection study – An analysis, usually provided by bank consultants (for a fee) using a statistical model supplied by Phoenix-Hecht, that provides optimal locations for company lockbox sites.

commercial paper – A negotiable, discount note issued by industrial firms, finance companies, utilities, and bank holding companies for maturities up to 270 days.

compensating balances – Amount of available (collected) balances bank customers must maintain in accounts to compensate for bank service charges and/or credit arrangements.

concentration account – Account used as central point for all incoming or outgoing movement of funds from other corporate accounts. This account may also be the same thing as a Master Account (see below).

confirmed letter of credit – A letter of credit that guarantees all drafts drawn against it.

confirming bank – A bank that has been authorized or requested by an issuing bank in a letter of credit transaction to confirm the issuing bank's irrevocable letter of credit. This is a second assurance of payment and is used if the beneficiary has any doubts about the issuing bank's ability to pay the letter of credit.

controlled disbursement – A bank service that provides the total amount of daily check clearings to customers early on the same (business) day that the checks clear so that the customer can fund the disbursement account that (same) day.

corporate trade payments – Payments made by one corporation to another, usually via electronic commerce/electronic data interchange through the ACH.

correspondent bank – A domestic (U.S.) bank or a bank in a foreign country that provides payment and other services (e.g. settlement, check clearing, account processing, etc.) for another bank; often done on a reciprocal basis.

custody – A bank service that maintains investment securities for customers. The service tracks and delivers securities that are bought and sold, handles dividends that may be payable, and often reports the status of the investment portfolio to the customer.

daylight overdraft – The intra-day net debit (or overdraft) position of a bank that creates a credit exposure for the Federal Reserve, which guarantees finality of all Fedwire transfers and would have to fund the bank overdraft if it is not resolved by the end of the business day. In order to control risk, the Federal Reserve has instituted a policy limiting the amount of daylight overdrafts for banks.

demand deposit – Funds that are available to the customer at any time, require no advance notice of withdrawal, and may be accessed by check or wire transfer. Checking accounts, often referred to as demand deposit accounts (DDAs) are the most common form of demand deposit.

deposit reconciliation or consolidation – A bank service that combines deposits made at multiple branches (of that same bank) but which retains information on the individual deposit locations and the deposit amounts. This information can be transmitted to the customer via the bank's information reporting system.

deposit cutoff – The time at which a bank lockbox operator will close out the daily deposit(s), usually agreed to by the customer and the bank.

direct debit – A method of collecting funds from a customer's account using the ACH, for which the customer has given prior approval.

direct deposit – An ACH transaction used to make payments for payroll and other employee payments into the employee's bank account.

direct send – The term used when a bank sends a batch of checks directly to a correspondent, to the bank on which the checks are drawn, or to the Federal Reserve. The purpose is to clear checks faster than depositing them with the sending bank's local Federal Reserve.

documentary collection – A common form of international trade transaction in which a seller retains title to goods sold internationally until it has received payment, which is processed by a bank's (or third party's) inspection and approval of the documentation associated with the transaction.

draft – A check-like payment instrument that is used in international trade (with letters of credit). It can be a *sight draft* (payable upon demand) or *time draft* (payable at a preset future date).

drawee bank – The bank on which a check is drawn and to which it must be presented to collect funds.

earnings credit rate (ECR) – The rate used by a bank to calculate the value of collected balances (after reserve requirements) maintained by customers and usually tied to a money market rate or prescribed rate set by the bank. It is stated as an annual rate but applied on a monthly basis.

e-commerce (electronic commerce) – The exchange of information in an electronic medium by two businesses, including such means as fax, electronic data interchange transactions, Internet transactions, and computer-to-computer transactions, directly or via the Internet.

EDI (electronic data interchange) – The electronic interchange of business data between trading partners in a standard format. It is a type of e-commerce.

EFT (electronic funds transfer) – The transfer of value from one bank to another using automated, non-paper-based means, such as the ACH system or Fedwire.

encoded amount – The dollar amount of the check that appears in the MICR line of a check and is added by the bank of first deposit or added by the depositor prior to deposit.

euro – The common currency for most of the European Common Market.

Eurodollars – Funds (i.e., US $) in foreign banks or foreign branches of US banks. The prefix "Euro" is used to designate that the currency has been created outside of the home country for the currency, as in Euroyen or Eurosterling.

Fed – See *Federal Reserve Board*

Fed float – The time that elapses between the Federal Reserve's granting availability and the actual time it takes the Federal Reserve to clear the check to the drawee bank.

Fed funds – Reserves (funds in their account with the Federal reserve) traded among banks. It is also used to mean immediately available or same-day funds when requesting immediate funds transfers.

Federal agency issues – Short-term securities issued by agencies of U.S. government, such as Federal Home Loan Bank notes.

Federal Reserve Board – The central monetary authority of the United States that was created by the Federal Reserve Act of 1913.

Federal Reserve System – The central bank of the United States created by Congress and consisting of a seven member Board of Governors in Washington, D.C., 12 regional Reserve Banks, 25 Federal Reserve branches, regional check processing centers, and member depository financial institutions (commercial banks).

Fedwire – An electronic network run by the Fed connecting the Federal Reserve banks, the U.S. Treasury, various government agencies, and member banks that is used to transfer funds.

float – The status of check payments that are in the process of being collected (or cleared) through the banking system. Depositors of checks experience collection float, which delays their use of the funds deposited (see availability). Drawers of the checks can maintain use of the funds needed to cover the checks issued until the checks occur (see controlled disbursements).

foreign exchange – The buying and selling of currencies worldwide.

foreign exchange exposure – The potential loss that could be suffered if foreign exchange rates were to change adversely, either from a transaction involving two different currencies or from translating the foreign assets of a company back to its home currency.

144

Forward FX contract – A transaction in which a company completes a transaction with its bank for a sale or purchase of foreign currency that matures longer than one or two days, depending on the currency.

giro system – A central bill paying system used for consumer payments, primarily in Europe, that is often operated by the governmental postal services in each country.

high order sort – A way to organize disbursement accounts so that multiple locations can draw checks on the same account. The first three digits usually designate the location. Periodic reconciliation reports are prepared for each location and can be distributed to each location. This service obviates the need for additional small-volume accounts. It may also be call *subaccounting*.

High Dollar Group Sort – A Federal Reserve program to accelerate the clearing time of checks drawn on high volume clearing points (those with >$10 million in daily clearing) by allowing the Federal Reserve to make two presentments (no later than noon for the second one) of checks to be cleared instead of the normal single presentment.

Image replacement document (IRD) – An electronically digitized version of a paper check. The digitized check images can be cleared electronically. See also Check 21 and remote capture/deposit.

imaging – A technology that forms a digital picture of an object, such as a check or piece of paper and transmits this picture to a computer file.

information reporting system – A bank service that consolidates daily balance and activity information for one or more bank accounts prior to opening of business and during the business day and reports the information to the user by means of a communications link, such as a modem hook-up or through the Internet.

issuing bank – The bank that opens a letter of credit, thereby extending its guarantee and promise to pay the letter of credit beneficiary if the prescribed terms and conditions are met.

kiting – Attempting to draw against non-existent funds or to "create" funds by drawing against float for fraudulent purposes.

ledger balance – see *Book balance.*

letter of credit (L/C, or LOC) – A financial instrument issued by a bank on behalf of an individual or corporation by which the bank substitutes its own credit for that of the individual or corporation to provide financial assurance (a standby letter) or financial support for an underlying trade transaction (commercial letter).

LIBOR (London InterBank Offered Rate) – The rate set daily among banks in the London (Eurodollar) market. Short-term LIBOR rates are often used as base reference rates for short-term bank loans and as base rates in other financial transactions, such as interest rate risk management derivative instruments.

line of credit – A borrowing arrangement that a bank offers to a corporation or individual that represents the maximum dollar amount of loans that the borrower may incur (i.e., have outstanding at any point) over a period of time, usually up to one year.

lockbox – A collection mechanism by which mail containing customer payments is sent directly to a post office box address that is serviced by a bank or third party.

mail float – The time a check is in the mail from the customer to the receipt by the company or its lockbox processor.

magnetic ink character recognition (MICR) – Magnetic characters that are encoded at the bottom of a check that permit use of automated equipment in the bank clearing process. The characters appear on the MICR line (see below).

master account – The account to which all activity is transferred from related ZBAs and which provides funds to offset any deficits in the individual ZBA accounts. A master account may also function as a company's concentration account.

MICR line – The line at the bottom of a paper check that contains information for check clearing in magnetic-character form.

MICR option – An automated service provided by lockbox banks to provide the data in the MICR line of a check to the customer.

National Automated Clearing House Association (NACHA) – The national association that establishes the standards, rules and procedures that enable depository financial institutions to exchange automated clearing house payments on a national basis.

negotiating bank – A bank that examines documents under an export letter of credit and arranges to pay the beneficiary of the letter of credit.

next-day settlement – The settlement of ACH transactions at the start of business on the day following their processing date. This is the earliest time in which ACH transactions can be settled, except for ACH transfers within the same bank's system.

OCC (Office of the Comptroller of the Currency) – U.S. federal agency that oversees national banks and is responsible for issuing bank charters and examining national banks.

on-us – Entries within an ACH file destined to accounts held at the Originating Depository Financial Institution that remain at that bank and are not transmitted any further.

on-us checks – Checks that are deposited and presented for payment at the same bank on which the check is drawn, usually resulting in immediately available funds.

Originating Depository Financial Institution (ODFI) – A participating ACH member that initiates (or has initiated for it) ACH debit and/or credit entries that it transmits directly or indirectly to its ACH system operator.

payable-through draft – Legal, check-like instruments, drawn on and paid by the issuer (rather than the bank), which serves only as an agent in the clearing process with the drafts flowing through it to the issuer for its examination and final payment authorization. Payable-through-drafts are treated like checks.

payee – The party who accepts the check or to whom the check or payment is made out/drawn.

payor – The party who writes a check or payment.

point of sale – The direct electronic transfer of funds information between the customer's and merchant's accounts via electronic terminals, communication, and computer facilities. It can also refer to the merchant's location of business where such a transaction may take place.

pooling – A cash concentration technique offered by banks in some foreign countries. It nets the opening balances (daily) for all accounts associated with the same customer and within that country, with only the net amount across all linked accounts being assessed overdraft interest and charges or receiving interest from the bank.

positive pay– A bank service whereby the bank verifies key information on a check, usually check number and dollar amount, against a file provided by the customer prior to accepting it for payment. Any checks that do not agree are held for a fixed but short period of time until the bank receives instructions from the customer.

post dated – A future-dated payment instrument, usually a check, which is negotiable on the date specified.

preauthorized payment (electronic) – An ACH service that permits a customer to agree in advance for payment of a bill to a company or bank to be electronically withdrawn from the customer's account.

prenotification (prenote) – An optional, zero-dollar paperless transaction that alerts the receiving financial institution that the originating company has obtained an authorization from a customer and that future paperless entries will be submitted for or against the customer's account.

presentment – The actual delivery of a check (or other negotiable instrument) by a bank clearing agent to the drawee bank for payment or acceptance.

purchasing card (p-card) – A service provided by a bank or nonbank card issuer that allows companies to issue cards similar to credit cards, but with limits on purchasing dollar amounts and restricted choice of suppliers. Companies using purchasing cards are liable for all amounts charged against the card. Also referred to as procurement cards.

Receiving Depository Financial Institution (RDFI) – Any financial institution qualified to receive debits and credits through its regional ACH.

recourse – The right to demand payment from the endorser of a check when the first party liable fails to pay. Also applies to a negotiating bank's right to reclaim funds paid to a letter of credit beneficiary in the event payment is not obtained from the issuing bank.

regional check processing centers (RCPC) – Processing centers whose operation is similar to the check processing and collection system maintained at each Federal Reserve Bank and branch but intended to service a smaller group of banks within a given geographic area, not located in a Federal Reserve district or branch city.

reimbursing bank – A specified bank designated and authorized by a letter of credit issuing bank to pay funds from the issuing bank's account to either a designated paying or accepting bank or to any bank authorized to negotiate the issuing bank's letter of credit.

remittance advice – Information on a check stub or on an accompanying or attached document (such as an invoice) by the payor that tells the payee why a payment is being made.

Remote capture/deposit – The process of scanning checks to convert them to electronic, digitized records that can be transmitted to a bank of the check receiver's choice. Banks also use this process to clear checks from branches and/or lockbox service departments.

repurchase agreement (repo) – A short-term investing arrangement in which a dealer sells a security to an investor with the agreement to buy it back at a specified price usually at a specific future date, during which time the investor owns the securities outright.

reserve requirement – The portion of customer deposits that member banks must keep on deposit at the Federal Reserve and which banks charge back to their customers by deducting them from the customer's collected balance. It is currently 10% for demand deposits (checking accounts) and is set by the Fed.

retail lockbox – A lockbox system designed to process large volumes of small-size payments, usually accompanied by a machine-readable document.

return document – A paper advice, check stub, or voucher returned with the remitted check to a retail lockbox.

returned item - A check or ACH debit sent to another bank for collection and payment that is returned unpaid to the depositing bank.

reverse positive pay – A service similar to positive pay (see above), except that the bank transmits a file of checks to be paid, and the customer verifies that they are in agreement with the customer's issuance file. This service is usually used by larger firms that have their own in-house reconciliation systems.

reverse repo – A short-term liquidity transaction in which an investor holding a security under a repo uses the underlying security as backing for a short-term loan. These are often done with the dealer with whom the repo was made.

revolving credit agreement (revolver) – A line of bank credit that includes a legal agreement and which can be negotiated for longer period of time than regular lines of credit, often done with more than one bank.

safekeeping – See *custody*.

same-day funds – Funds deposited in an account that are immediately available to the depositor.

serial number – The check number

signature card – A card signed for each bank account that documents authorized signers and enables the bank to verify signatures on checks and other documents, if this is arranged.

Single European Payment Area (SEPA) – An electronic payment system for euro payments inn Europe.

spot FX trade – A trade between a company and its bank for the sale or purchase of a foreign currency. A spot trade takes effect in one day (for North America) or two days (for other currencies) for U.S. transactions.

stale-dated check – A check that is six months or more older prior to its presentation (as indicated by its date).

stop payment – A customer's instruction to the payor bank to refuse payment of a specified check that has been drawn on the customer's account and return the check if it is presented for payment. Stop payments can be made via bank information system or by telephone communication and may be in force for finite but renewable periods of time, such as six months.

sweep arrangement – A bank service where all the funds above a specified amount are automatically transferred out of an account, invested overnight, and automatically transferred into the account the following morning, or as needed.

SWIFT (Society for Worldwide Interbank Financial Telecommunication) – A private telecommunications service established and owned by a group of banks worldwide to provide member institutions with a common data transmission network worldwide.

t-bills – See *U.S. Treasury Bills*.

transit/routing number – A nine-digit number that identifies a specific financial institution and facilitates check collection by the Federal Reserve and other banks. Also referred to as the ABA Transit/Routing Number or the ABA number.

treasury work station – A special type of software for handling treasury management applications that retrieves data from banks and other information sources, consolidates and stores it in a data base, provides reporting and analytical capabilities, and usually a link to the company's accounting system. Most of the providers of treasury work stations are non-bank companies.

truncation – See *check truncation*.

UCC (Uniform Commercial Code) – The underlying law in the U.S. for commercial transactions. UCC provides basic legal definitions and rules for bank check processing and electronic funds transfer and other transactions. UCC is adopted by individual states but with common provisions.

uncommitted line of credit – A line of credit offered by a bank to its customer that may be withdrawn at any time prior to any loan transaction.

unbundling – A trend in banking where banks itemize their service charges on customer account analysis statements by charging separately for each component of the cash management services provided.

uncollected funds – That portion of a deposit balance not yet collected by the depository bank, essentially the same thing as float.

U.S. Treasury Bills(t-bills) – A short-term security issued by the U.S. government through weekly sales of three- and six-month maturities so that bills maturing each week up to six months are available in the secondary market. These are considered the most risk-free short-term security.

value dating – A technique used by banks in some countries to defer availability of funds deposited or disbursed.

wholesale lockbox – A form of bank lockbox service that is characterized by small volumes of large-dollar checks.

wire transfer – A transaction by which funds are moved from one bank to another electronically, usually through the Fedwire system.

zero balance account (ZBA) – A subsidiary account whose balance is adjusted to zero at the end of each bank processing day by transferring the amount offset as a debit or credit to a single master account within the bank. ZBAs are more often used for disbursements than deposits. Otherwise, a ZBA account functions like an ordinary checking account.

ZBA arrangement – The overall organization of master account and subordinate ZBA accounts within the same bank.

About the Author

Kenneth L. Parkinson is managing director of Treasury Information Services, LLC, a consulting and publishing firm, and has served as a visiting and adjunct associate professor at Stern Graduate School of Business at New York University where he teaches courses in working capital management, corporate finance, and corporate treasury practices. He actively consults with organizations of all sizes on treasury management projects. He is a frequent speaker at major industry conferences and seminars given by the New York Institute of Finance, the American Institute of Certified Public Accountants, and the American Management Association and is one of the leading authorities on corporate treasury practice.

Ken is the author or co-author of *Optimizing Bank Relations*, *How to Prepare an RFP for Bank Services*, *Corporate Liquidity*, *Treasury Manager's Guide to the Internet*, and *Cash Management Templates*. and is a frequent author of articles in trade magazines. He is a contributing author for *The Corporate Cash Management Handbook*. He is currently on the editorial board of the *Journal of Corporate Treasury Management* and has served as senior editor with *Business Credit* magazine, contributing and technology editor for *Corporate Cashflow* magazine, co-editor of the *TMAC News* and *TMAC Journal* (now the *Canadian Treasurer*), the *Treasury Pro*, *TMA News*, and editor-in-chief of the *Journal of Cash Management*.

Previously, Ken was director of treasury operations at RCA Corporation, managing treasury and banking activities worldwide. He holds a B.S. from Penn State and an M.B.A. from the Wharton Graduate School (University of Pennsylvania) and is a permanently certified cash manager (CCM).

Treasury Information Services, LLC specializes in helping organizations update financial and treasury procedures and technology as well as select and manage banking relationships. It provides consulting and training services to companies of all sizes, government agencies, and not-for-profit organizations as well as to banks and other service providers. Through TIS Publishing, it publishes books that are widely acknowledged to be insightful, practical, and eminently useful. (See last page for information on ordering.)

Preparing for Cash Management Certification

This self-study guide includes detailed reviews, test-taking tips, study aids, and over 400 original practice questions and problems. It is revised and kept up-to- date with the current version of the body of knowledge. $89.95

RFP Questionnaires for Financial Services

70 separate questionnaires for financial services including custody services, remote capture of checks, short-term lines of credit, commercial letters of credit, pay cards, and more. Includes advice about creating an RFP package and understanding price estimates. $144.00 elec/$149.00CD-ROM

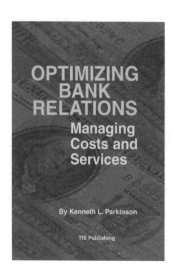

OPTIMIZING
BANK
RELATIONS
Managing
Costs and
Services

By Kenneth L. Parkinson

TIS Publishing

Optimizing Bank Relations

This is the only book that covers all aspects of a key treasury responsibility. It shows you how to calculate your real banking costs, understand your account analysis, negotiate fair compensation, and measure bank service performance. You also get more than 36 specialized tracking forms. $35.00

TIS Quick Order Form

Fax: 609-466-0091
Tel:1-888-TIS-BOOK
(847-2665) toll free
E-mail orders:
books@tisconsulting.com

Mail orders: TIS Publishing, P.O. Box 99, Hopewell, NJ 08525

Please send me the following books
(I understand that I may return my unmarked book(s) for a full refund.)

Qty.	Title	Price	Total
___	Managing Your Cash Position	$39.95	$ _____
___	Preparing for Cash Mgmt Certification	$89.95	$ _____
___	RFP Quest. for Financial Svcs. (elec)	$144.00	$ _____
	(note: no shipping fee)		
___	RFP Quest. for Financial Svcs. (CD)	$149.00	$ _____
___	Optimizing Bank Relations	$35.00	$ _____
	Please add 7% sales tax for books sent to NJ		$_____

Shipping (US): $5.00 for one book; $10.00
for 2-6 books; **Outside US:** contact office $_____

                    Total enclosed or charged $_____

Please send information about: [ ] Consulting [ ] Training

Name:_____

Tel:_____ E-mail:_____

Firm:_____ Dept: _____

Street:_____ Mail Code:_____

City:_____ State:_____ ZIP:_____

Payment: Credit card: [ ] MasterCard [ ] Visa [ ] AmEx [ ] Check enclosed

Card no.: _____ Sec. code_____

Name on card: _____Exp. date:_____

Billing address for card:_____

City:_____State:_____ ZIP:_____